VENTURE WI

G. I. GURDJIEFF

VENTURE
WITH IDEAS

KENNETH WALKER

LUZAC
ORIENTAL

Second edition, revised, published by
Luzac Oriental Ltd,
46 Great Russell Street, London WC1,
January 1995

First published
by Jonathan Cape, London, May 1951

ISBN 1 898942 04 8 HARDBACK
ISBN 1 898942 05 6 PAPERBACK

Printed and bound in Great Britain by
Biddles Limited, Guildford and Kings Lynn

CONTENTS

To that arch-disturber of self-complacency,
the late G. I. GURDJIEFF

FOREWORD

IF Kenneth Walker were alive today, some forty years after the first publication of *Venture with Ideas*, he would be happy and reassured to find that the work that G. I. Gurdjieff brought, far from ending with his death in 1949 as some feared, is very much alive. During this time it has rooted itself in the minds and hearts of many people in many countries. Amongst these are some – alas in declining numbers – who lived close to Gurdjieff during the final decade of his life. But there are also many younger people who, although they did not know him in his lifetime, have nevertheless responded with conscience to the enduring presence of his ideas, and wished to explore the path that he opens to us.

Today Gurdjieff's teaching is like a powerful stream flowing directly across the world with an intensity so strong that the fact of having known or not known Gurdjieff in his lifetime is of little account. There is no rift or separation between the various generations that have succeeded each other in studying his ideas over the past half-century.

At the present time *Venture with Ideas* has a double significance, it is temporal and timeless. On the one hand, the book faithfully describes a certain epoch in the life of the work to which Walker himself belonged. On the other, it speaks of ideas which are the patrimony of Higher Knowledge and which represent an endowment and reason of mankind far beyond the usual intellectual modes of thought.

Thus, to be this enlivened by reading a sincere and authentic narrative, such as the one Kenneth Walker gives us, is a witness and guarantee of its vivifying power on the generation to come. Its place lies mid-way between the warmth of the oral transmission of a teaching, which is both indispensable and impossible to describe, and the coldness of an analytic and didactic text, which is exact and useful, but lacks the power to communicate a direct vibration of life.

It is a great privilege for me to have been asked to write an introduction to a new edition of a book of this quality. The memory of having sat with Kenneth Walker at Mr Gurdjieff's table and of having worked with him at a later date in some groups in London, allows me to see clearly how his fundamental honesty and fine critical mind, together with his love of effort and adventure, combine to constitute the hallmark of this essence-friend.

Bernard Courtenay-Mayers, M.C., M.D.
London, October 1994.

INTRODUCTION

THIS book requires an explanation and it is in the introduction that this should be given. In 1946 my publishers were good enough to re-issue a book of mine which, written and published several years previously under the title *The Intruder*, was both out of print and out of date. It reappeared under a fresh name after having been largely rewritten. To cursory readers the new book, *I Talk of Dreams*, appeared to be only a rather light-hearted autobiography, but those with more discernment realized that its autobiographical details were only incidental and that it was primarily a study in psychology. My motive in writing it was clearly enunciated on the first page, where the following passage occurred: 'This book is a record of some of the writer's own mechanisms. Like a teacher of biology I illustrate the laws of living by showing them at work on the actual animal, but in this case I am not only the demonstrator but the object which he demonstrates. In short, I am my own rabbit.' A condition had been attached by Jonathan Cape to the re-issuing of my former work, namely, that it should be brought up to date; instead of ending in 1925, as *The Intruder* had done, the new book should end in the year 1946.

What could be more reasonable and natural than this condition and yet it was one which it was impossible for me to fulfil. In 1923 I met a man who was destined to exert an immense influence over my life, P. D. Ouspensky, the author of *Tertium Organum* and *A New Model of the Universe*. Ouspensky was well known as a writer, but what was not generally known was that he was also the exponent of a special system of knowledge which he had previously learnt from Gurdjieff. I attended the private meetings at which he expounded this teaching from 1923 till 1947, the year of his death, and I gave him the promise which he exacted of all his followers, namely, that nothing that was learnt at his meetings should be spoken about in public and allowed to appear in print. How then could I possibly bring my autobiography up to date and at the

9

same time leave out of it what was of such great importance to me, the system of knowledge I had obtained from Ouspensky? My publishers, without knowing the real reason for my difficulty, were so considerate as to rescue me from the dilemma in which I found myself by waiving the condition they had made.

The recent publication of Ouspensky's and Gurdjieff's books, *In Search of the Miraculous* and *All and Everything*, have now freed me from my old promise and I am at liberty to reveal what previously had to be kept silent. There is no further need for me to stop abruptly in the development of a line of thought because it begins to encroach on ideas I learnt from Ouspensky. I am no longer obliged to erase from time to time what I have already written on the grounds that it has a too close affinity to Ouspensky's teaching. For the first time in well-nigh thirty years I am free to write whatever I care to write and I am conscious of a new and unaccustomed sense of freedom. In my opinion the system of knowledge taught by Ouspensky and Gurdjieff is of such value that it merits the widest possible publicity, and it is this conviction of mine which has prompted me to write this present book. I have called it *Venture with Ideas* on the grounds that a venture is an enterprise on which the adventurer sets out without being able to foretell what will be its outcome. The voyage of discovery on which I embarked light-heartedly nearly thirty years ago was certainly of this nature and it has proved to be as rich in unexpected incidents and hazards as the journey I made as a younger man through what at that time was a little-known part of Africa. For it is a grave mistake to look upon ideas as passive instruments of the mind which we can use for a period and then, when we have grown tired of them, throw aside. They are powerful agents capable of taking possession of us and of propelling us in a direction in which, at the beginning, we had no desire to go. There are ideas so powerful indeed that they are capable of destroying us body and soul, as the speculations of Engels and Marx and the idea of the sanctity of the state have destroyed many men and women who have been rash enough to lend them their credence. It is because I now realize how potent are the ideas I received from Ouspensky and Gurdjieff that I look upon my past association with these two remarkable men as having been a great psychological hazard. *Venture with Ideas* is therefore an appropriate title for the book that is to follow.

INTRODUCTION

It is not my intention to give an account of Gurdjieff's system
of knowledge, and for two reasons. The first is that knowledge of
this kind is imparted orally and in accordance with the standing
of the pupil. The second is that those ideas in Gurdjieff's system of
knowledge which are of a more general nature have already been
published in Ouspensky's book, *In Search of the Miraculous,* and in
Gurdjieff's own allegorical work, *All and Everything.* It is to these
that the reader must therefore turn if he requires more detailed
information on the subject of Gurdjieff's teaching. I have a different
object in writing this book. It is to give an account of the impact of
this knowledge on a man who had received an orthodox scientific
education and who was in no way a searcher for esoteric truth, the
man in question being myself. The very term 'esoteric truth' would
have elicited a smile or a shrug of the shoulders had it been uttered
in my presence prior to my meeting with Ouspensky. Like Bertrand
Russell, a far cleverer person than myself, I believed that the scientific method was the only instrument by which it was possible to
discover truth. The idea that there existed an underground trickle
of knowledge which from time to time made its way to the surface
and then plunged underground again would have appeared to
me to be utterly fantastic. Yet when I now look back at the history
of Western knowledge and note the appearance from time to time
of some teacher who gathers around him a circle of disciples,
imparts knowledge to them for a few years, and then either dies or
disappears, I see no way of explaining these events other than by
the term 'esoteric knowledge'. I am referring to such teachers as
Pythagoras, Appolonias of Tyana, Ammonius Sacca, the teacher of
Plotinus, St Martin, generally known as 'le philosophe inconnu', and
a long line of other men whose names have now been forgotten.
And the fact that the memory of these teachers of esoteric truth so
rapidly fades is the second and more important reason for my
undertaking this book. I wish to give an account of a modern representative of this long line of teachers, of a man known only to a
comparative few and who in his own book gives the following
description of himself. 'He who in childhood was called "Tatakh";
in early youth "Darky"; later "the Black Greek"; in middle age,
the "Tiger of Turkestan"; and now, not just anybody, but the
genuine "Monsieur" or "Mister" Gurdjieff, or the "nephew of
Prince Mukransky", or finally, simply a "Teacher of Dancing".'

It is therefore to Gurdjieff, the most astonishing man I have ever met, the man from whom I have learnt more than from any other person, that I dedicate this book. To end this foreword with the customary Latin tag, 'Requiescat in pace,' would be singularly inappropriate. To whatever sphere Gurdjieff's spirit has been called, it does not rest there, but continues instead the struggle which it began long ago upon earth, the struggle to reach a higher level of being.

Little London
1950

CHAPTER I

THE ARK-BUILDERS

This book is the chronicle of a journey through the bewildering inner world of ideas, a journey in which I was fortunate enough to have two remarkable men as guides. I would have liked to have described it as a search for real knowledge, but to have done so would have been presumptuous; it would be to claim an understanding that I did not initially possess but had to acquire. A search is a quest for something that is known to exist, but when I started out on this journey I had no idea that it was possible to find knowledge of a special kind. A mild curiosity and a readiness for adventure are all to which I can lay claim and it was fortunate that at the beginning these were enough. I owe everything that happened to good luck, to my friendship with M. and to the two men whom I met. The fateful words which started me off on this journey, the accident which altered the course of my life, were spoken at the junction of Weymouth Street and Harley Street. They were uttered by M. in the late afternoon of a day in the autumn of 1923. We had met by chance and we were both on our way to Oxford Circus.

'It's strange,' he said, 'that you should have just written a book on the voyage of the Ark. What made you do it?'

'Well, it seemed a good theme for a children's book,' I answered. 'And so it turned out to be. It almost wrote itself.' But why, I wondered, should M. think this strange and why had he suddenly introduced this subject when we had been talking about something entirely different? 'What makes you think it strange?' I asked.

'Because an ark is a symbol for a refuge in a time of trouble. Noah was warned of the disasters ahead; we also will require an ark in the time to come, and there is a small group of people now in London that has started building one.'

'What on earth —?'

He interrupted me. 'There are great disasters ahead of us and we've got to prepare for them. There will be wars, political unrest, revolutions, and all on such a scale that everything that humanity has managed to build up may well fall in ruins.'

He looked unusually stern as he uttered these words, but I was accustomed to his dramatic pronouncements and I was not going to allow myself to be disturbed by this sudden outburst of pessimism. 'I don't believe it,' I answered. 'Why, we've only just finished a war and everybody knows now that wars don't pay, even if you win them. The nations have learnt their lesson at last, and now, for the first time in history, steps are being taken to settle international disputes by other means than slaughter. The League of Nations is no longer an idealist's dream but an accomplished fact. At this moment in Geneva —'

M. gripped my arm so that I had to stop. Then he swung round and faced me. 'It won't work,' he said slowly, and with emphasis on each word. 'It cannot possibly work, and after a few years the League will not exist. So long as men remain as they are everything will continue as it has always been. All these leagues, covenants and plans, all these treaties and high-sounding words mean nothing, absolutely nothing. You don't believe me, K., but what I'm telling you is the truth.'

He had now let go my arm and we continued our way down the long length of Harley Street and across Cavendish Square. We walked in silence, for M. had spoken with such assurance that I could not avoid being impressed by what he had said. A soothing refrain about 'a war to end war' started up in my head, but it had no power to exorcise M.'s words. Was it possible that the Bolshevik revolution, or the great Russian experiment, as we now preferred to call it, would spread and destroy the whole structure of Europe? No, I refused to believe that the world was as mad as he had made it out to be. But he had spoken in a tone of authority that made me wonder whether he was aware of facts unknown to me. I must find out more. 'Who has prophesied all these disasters?' I asked just as we reached Oxford Street.

'Gurdjieff.'

It was a name I had heard only on two or three previous occasions and then uttered by him. A year ago M. had suddenly abandoned his practice and had gone off to France. I knew that he had been living in some sort of institute in a château near Fontainebleau from which he had only returned to London a few weeks ago. I knew also that while he had been abroad he had been engaged on some sort of strenuous work connected with a system of development. But he had been very reticent about what actually happened at the château. He had said something about the use of 'irritation and exhaustion' as a means of gaining control over oneself – whatever that enigmatical remark might mean. He had also mentioned, and with unusual respect, the name of the founder of the Institute, the name he had just uttered. He had described Gurdjieff as being a man possessed of immense knowledge and of unusual powers and had then apparently been on the point of adding something more but had changed his mind. My only other source of information concerning Gurdjieff was a short article that had appeared a few weeks previously in one of the illustrated daily papers. The article was entitled 'The Forest Philosophers' and it stated that there were a number of people of all nationalities living in a Fontainebleau château who were engaged in some sort of work under the guidance of a Caucasian Greek named Gurdjieff. Amongst those who had joined this colony – its full name was 'The Institute for the Harmonious Development of Man' – were Orage, the editor of the *New Age*, and Katherine Mansfield. Beyond informing me that Gurdjieff's pupils were building a large studio in which certain temple dances and complicated movements were to be performed, the article gave me very little new knowledge about the Institute. 'Is Gurdjieff in London now?' I asked. 'Is it he who is directing the people you spoke about, the people who are building an ark?'

'No, Gurdjieff is still in France, but Ouspensky is here. He's got a small group in London. Would you like to go to one of his meeting? It's by special invitation only, but I think I could get permission for you to go.'

A group, a circle of devoted followers, mostly women, gathered round a teacher who was doubtless under the guidance of a Master living in Tibet – it did not attract me. Wars were always followed by an outbreak of spiritualistic or esoteric groups. There was one such group which met in the neighbourhood of Queen's Gate and which practised spiritual healing under the inspired guidance of a bus conductor and an ex-postman. But I had heard Ouspensky's name before. He was the author, so far as I could remember, of a book that had made rather a hit in America. I would certainly like to meet him, but privately, and not under the condition of joining a group. I was on the point of thanking M. for his offer and of explaining to him that, at the moment, I was so fully occupied in the evenings that it would be better for me to defer attending Ouspensky's meetings when a new thought entered my mind. If M. had come across ideas that appeared to him to be of such value that he had abandoned his practice for a year in order to study them, surely they were worthy of my own investigation, even at the expense of joining a group. I reversed the decision I had previously reached.

'Thank you very much, M. I'd like to go if it can be managed.'

'All right. I'll let you know.'

We had now reached Oxford Circus where we were to part. I plunged into Oxford Circus tube station while he went on to Regent Street to keep an appointment. It is thus that important decisions in our lives are made, casually and light-heartedly and without any realization of their significance. A chance meeting, a few words uttered accidentally, a thought suddenly coming into the mind when one is about to enter a London tube and the whole future of one's life is changed either for better or for worse.

M. telephoned to me a few days later and on the Thursday of the following week I found myself searching for a number on the badly illuminated front doors of the houses of Warwick Gardens. At last I found the right number and in the company of two other people entered a small hall. Seated in it, at a tiny table, sat a lady who ticked off our names on a list. She had the high cheekbones of the Russian, friendly eyes, and, from the remark she made to my companions, I was convinced that she also possessed a keen sense of humour. No better person could have been placed at the doorway to a new and very doubtful adventure so far as I was concerned. I was considerably reassured and felt that joining a group might not be quite so bad as I had expected it to be.

The room we now entered was furnished only with a large number of small chairs facing a blackboard and a small table on which rested an empty tumbler, a carafe of water, a brass ashtray, a duster and a box of chalks. There was one small oil painting on the walls, and on the window-sill stood a vase containing a few sprigs of artificial cherry-blossom made out of shells. In twos and threes more and more people trickled into the room, but even when it was well past the time for the meeting to begin, there was still no sign of Mr Ouspensky. A few members of the audience whispered to each other, but the great majority sat in their chairs – how uncomfortable the chairs were – looking straight in front of them, or else down at their feet. I was carried back to the presbyterian churches of my boyhood, so strongly was I reminded of a Scottish congregation awaiting the arrival of the minister. I decided to spend the time examining more carefully the fellow-members of my group. These builders of an ark looked intelligent on the whole, but none of them excited my curiosity. The two sexes were about equally represented and the great majority of those present were middle-aged. Only six people in the audience could be considered youthful and I wondered what reason had induced them to come here. Although I could not be certain of this, I was fairly sure that the motive that had brought most of those present into this austere and rather dreary room in Kensington was disillusionment. They were disappointed both with what life had to offer them and probably also with themselves. Formerly such people would have found solace in the church, but in this scientific and sceptical age men and women had lost faith in the resources of religion and were forced to seek for comfort elsewhere. Ouspensky probably provided them with what they needed, some outside interest that diverted their attention from themselves. In my opinion this would explain the presence of the great bulk of the audience, but not that of the people still in their twenties. Surely life provided all that these young people required, and surely they had no need to come here in search of an anodyne. My thoughts about the younger members of the audience were interrupted for the door behind had opened and now a very solid man of medium height, with closely cropped grey hair, was making his way to the vacant chair in front of me. He sat down without seeming to notice the audience, drew from his coat pocket a small sheet of paper and scrutinized it carefully. He was wearing very strong glasses, but instead of availing himself of them, he held the paper a few inches from his face and peered at it over the top of the lenses. Then he put his notes on the table, turned his attention to his audience, and said: 'Well?'

I had expected somebody quite different from the man who was now looking at us, but who was apparently in no hurry to begin his lecture. I had heard that Ouspensky was a mystic, but the man in front of me looked anything but that. I would have guessed him to be a scientist, or a lawyer, or at any rate somebody with his feet planted securely on firm ground. A minute passed and then without any introductory remarks or change of expression he plunged straight into his lecture. I found it difficult to follow him partly because he spoke with so marked a Russian intonation that one had the impression that one was listening to an unknown language. He made no use of gestures or of the other aids employed by lecturers, but this absence of all art in his delivery proved to be an asset. The very baldness of his statements added weight to them and disarmed all adverse criticism. One felt that he had no desire to wheedle his audience into believing whatever he chose to tell them but that he preferred to bring to its notice a number of ideas and then to leave it to his hearers to decide whether these ideas were valid or not. I had been right; he not only looked like a scientist, but he treated the subject-matter of his lecture as a scientist would treat it.

I shall make no attempt to reproduce Ouspensky's diction, but shall report what he said as clearly as I can. However obscure his speech might occasionally become, there could be no doubt that his mind was both orderly and clear. He began by saying that man attributed to himself a great many qualities that he did not actually possess. He believed that he had a permanent self, a master 'I', which integrated and controlled his thoughts, his emotions and his actions. This was an illusion, for if one turned one's attention inwards one would soon discover that instead of there being a single 'I', there were innumerable 'I's, many of which said contradictory things. All that one saw when one watched one's inner psychic processes was an endless procession of thoughts, sensations, imaginings and emotions, but nothing that could possibly be called a permanent and sovereign self. At this point he rose, walked to the blackboard and drew on it a large circle. He then subdivided this circle into a great many small areas by means of transverse and vertical lines. What he drew looked like the picture of a fly's eye seen under the microscope, a convex surface with thousands of different facets. In each facet he placed an 'I', and when he had completed his diagram, he announced: 'This is a picture of man. He has innumerable "I"s that are always changing. One "I" is

there at one moment and at the next it is replaced by another.'
Then he returned to his seat, sat down and invited questions.

'How long does an "I" last?' asked somebody.

'It is impossible to say. Every thought, every desire, every sensation says "I", and having said it disappears into the background. And what makes everything still more confusing is that these ephemeral "I"s don't know each other. A man decides in the evening to reform his habits and to get up early in the morning. But the "I" that wakes up next day knows nothing about any such plan and has no intention of rising any earlier than usual.'

'Aren't any of them connected?'

'All of them are in some way connected but we don't usually know the connections.'

'What then gives us the impression that we are permanent and one?' asked a rather thoughtful man with a grave and intelligent face.

'The fact that we have a body and a name. The body changes but so slowly that we are not aware of its changing. We go through life bearing always the same name. These two possessions of ours produce an illusion of unity and permanence. But this is only one of the many false ideas we have about ourselves.'

'What are the others?' asked the same questioner.

'We shall speak of that now,' answered Mr Ouspensky. 'A man also prides himself on being self-conscious, whereas even a short course of self-study will reveal the fact that one is very rarely aware of oneself, and then only for a few fleeting moments. Man believes that he has will, that he can "do", but this is also untrue. Everything happens in us in the same way that changes in the weather happen. Just as it rains, it snows, it clears up and it is fine, so also, within us, it likes, or it does not like, it is pleased, or it is distressed. We are machines set in motion by external influences, by impression reaching us from the outside world.' Having delivered himself of this chilly message, Ouspensky looked at his audience and smiled. Then he asked whether anybody would like to comment on this.

A heavy silence brooded over the room. There was nothing revolutionary for me in what Ouspensky had said, but he had expressed the idea of the automatism of man in a rather novel way. I had always accepted the possibility that man had no free will and that he was at the mercy of his desires and emotions, but I had always pictured him as a definite entity which was pulled this way and that by his changing moods. Mr Ouspensky had gone much further than this. He had denied that there was anything in man stable or persistent enough to have moods. According to him, man was only a sequence of dissolving views, a procession of isolated thoughts, sensations, perceptions and emotions. He was a chain of events, or inner responses to impressions reaching him from the outside world. Yet even that was not entirely new, for Hume had said something very like it. I would look up the passage in Hume when I got home. The silence in the room was becoming more and more uncomfortable, so oppressive that I was forced to break it.

'Isn't this idea than man is only a machine the view of the behaviourist school of psychology?' I asked. 'It seems to me to be only another way of saying that he is a chain of reflexes.'

Ouspensky looked at me. 'For them,' he said, 'it is only a convenient theory which they fail to apply to themselves and to their own mental constructions. They see automatism in others, but not in themselves. For us it has got to become something far more real than this. Unless we realize with our whole being that we do not possess unity, consciousness and will we will make no attempt to acquire them.'

'If we accept what you tell us —' began someone, but Ouspensky interrupted him.

'Accept nothing,' he said. 'Faith is not wanted here. Submit everything you hear from me to a personal test, to the test of self-observation. Find out whether it is true that you have no permanent or controlling self. Find out whether you can do things in a different way from that in which you have always done them, and when you have made your experiments, report your results. To accept something on trust, when you can prove it or disprove it, is laziness. Make your own experiments, and when you are in any doubt about them, ask questions.'

'What about art?' asked a lady with a very sensitive face. 'I can believe that what you say is true of most of our activities, I mean that they are mechanical. But art is an activity of man's spirit and his spirit is free. In speaking of art I am referring, of course, to the work of the great masters – Leonardo da Vinci, Michelangelo, and so on.'

'They also were machines,' he replied, 'very fine machines no doubt, but machines. There is such a thing as conscious and objective art, but we do not know it. All the art that we know is mechanical and subjective, even that of the old masters.'

'What distinction then do you make between the work of genius and the work of an ordinary man?'

'The same distinction that I make between the work of a very fine machine and that of an ordinary one. There are different kinds of machines; there are carts and wheelbarrows and there are calculating machines and aeroplanes.'

A small man wearing glasses now asked rather diffidently whether he might point out a difficulty. On being given permission he cleared his throat and said: 'A little time ago, Mr Ouspensky, you told us that we were not to accept what you said, but were to test it on ourselves. I think you mentioned self-observation.' Ouspensky nodded. 'Now, isn't there a danger of becoming too introspective if one does that? Doesn't one tend to think about oneself too much as it is?'

'I didn't say *think*, I said *see*,' he answered. 'Thinking – and by this you probably mean analysis – isn't wanted, for even if analysis does not begin in imagination, it always ends in it. Analysis comes much later. One simply observes oneself.'

'I thought you said that one hadn't got a self. So how can one observe what doesn't exist?' said a man who enunciated his words very clearly. He looked as though he might be either a schoolmaster or a lawyer.

'You confuse yourself with words,' Mr Ouspensky answered. 'Never mind about theories of having self or not having self. When one observes oneself all that one does is to turn the attention inwards and become a spectator of all one's activities. The French verb "constater" describes best what I mean. One registers everything instead of allowing it to pass unnoticed. One becomes aware of what formerly passed unnoticed.'

'Isn't that rather like self-analysis?' remarked somebody brightly.

'The very reverse. I've already said that analysis is not required,' answered Ouspensky. 'I say one thing, and then, a few moments afterwards, you say another. In the system of knowledge I teach you, use is made of a very exact language and before we can go any further this language must be studied.' He then proceeded to give very precise instructions for self-study. One was to look at oneself, at Mr A., or Mr B., or Mr C., or whoever one happened to be, as though looking at another person, noting without comment how he moved, thought and felt. Naturally one would discover in Mr A., or Mr B., or Mr C., things that one liked and things that one didn't like, but bad things should not be criticized, or good things approved. All that was required was to register everything as it happened, to become a spectator of one's various reactions. One thought that one knew oneself, but this was far from being true, and many discoveries would be made if one observed in the right way. Self-knowledge was the beginning of all wisdom, and self-study was a necessary preliminary to self-knowledge.

The lecture, if it can be called a lecture, lasted a little over an hour, and Mr Ouspensky frequently broke off during the course of it to invite questions. On several occasions no questions were asked, and then the atmosphere in the room became so heavy that one was often tempted to invent one. Only the lecturer seemed entirely undisturbed by these oppressive pauses but he appeared to be so detached from everything that I felt that even an explosion would fail to shake him. How imperturbable and impersonal he was, sitting there in his chair like something carved out of stone; so utterly different from the kind of man I had expected to meet. I had expected to find a mystic, a man who lived in a different world from the one I inhabited, but instead of encountering a dreamer, I had met a very solid scientist. Of one thing I was absolutely sure, that Ouspensky was as honest as he was unpretentious.

The lecture ended as suddenly as it had begun. After beckoning to somebody to follow him, Ouspensky rose and left the room. The strain of listening intently to his rather difficult English was suddenly released, and the sense of inner relief I experienced was apparently general. The audience immediately broke into a number of small groups and chattering began. As there was nobody to whom I could talk I made my way back into the hall and inquired of the Russian lady there whether there would be another meeting at the same time next week. 'There may be, or there may not be,' she replied with a smile. 'We can never be sure, but if you'll give me your telephone number, I'll let you know later.' People were now squeezing past me, making their way out of the building as she wrote down my telephone number. One of them failed to shut the front door after him, an omission that seemed to me to be of very little importance as others were just on the point of leaving. But Mr Ouspensky's secretary – I imagined she was this – immediately rose and spoke to four people conversing on the doorstep. 'Please disperse, and if you want to talk, do so somewhere else. You know that he doesn't want attention drawn to these meetings.' Having said this, she closed the door.

'Why this need for secrecy?' I wondered as I let myself out and shut the door carefully behind me. When M. had telephoned to tell me that he had permission for me to go to the meeting, he had added that one of the conditions for attendance was that nothing heard there should be mentioned to anybody else. Even the fact that meetings were being held in Warwick Gardens was to be kept quiet. There was nothing improper, blasphemous or illegal in these lectures, so why was it necessary to keep everything so quiet? All this secrecy seemed to me to be utterly absurd, and the more I thought about it, the less able I was to discover any reason for it. The meeting itself had certainly been interesting. I had been impressed by Ouspensky's clarity of thought, and more especially by the way he dealt with questions. However poor his English, he was always able to discern what was in his questioner's mind and to swoop on it with the unerring aim of a hawk. I liked his severity with any loose talk, and his contempt for the use of words as a substitute for thought. I also welcomed the absence of any sentimentality in what he said and felt that he was a man I could trust even when I did not agree with him. Of course the idea that a man was a machine was a very old one. It had been the theme of endless philosophical discussions, but Mr Ouspensky's method of dealing with it had been original. He argued that because man had no permanent self, but only a succession of changing 'I's, each of which exerted a momentary will, it was impossible for there to be a will for the whole man. He then approached the same subject from a different direction. He said that men were asleep, and then pointed out that in sleep we cannot exercise any control or will. If we wanted to be masters of ourselves, we must first awake, or to be more precise, we must attain self-awareness. This, he said, was a necessary preliminary to the acquirement of will.

But the more I clarified my ideas about Ouspensky, the more puzzled I became about his audience. What did the people I met in Warwick Gardens get from these meetings? Life was difficult for everybody, and still more difficult for men and women who thought. I had assumed that Ouspensky gave his followers the solace that in a former age they would have obtained from religion, but this was very unlikely. What comfort could these people get from the bleak gospel that he preached, the gospel that they were machines, had no will and that everything that happened in them was the result of external influence? Yet I gathered from the fragments of conversation I had overheard that some of them had been attending his lectures for several months. What help did they expect to get from his rather disturbing teaching? It was too early for me to be able to answer this question, and it was obvious that I must wait until I had attended more of his meetings.

CHAPTER II

OUR SEVERAL MINDS

THE next meeting was held a fortnight later, and before setting out for it I looked up the passage in Hume on the subject of the 'self'. Hume was the founder of a new psychological school of philosophy, and in his work he made great use of introspection, or what Mr Ouspensky preferred to call self-observation. The passage formed part of Hume's repudiation of Berkeley's view that every man had an 'intuitive knowledge' of his own soul, or self. 'For my part when I enter most intimately into what I call *myself*, I always stumble on some perception or other ... I never catch myself.' This was just what Ouspensky had said, and although I had not done enough self-observation to be dogmatic on the subject, Hume's statement appeared to me to be true. What one generally calls oneself turns out, on more careful observation, to be only a sequence of perceptions, emotions and thoughts. Was this shabby collection of psychic phenomena worthy of being called a soul or a self? If my soul were only the patchwork of cheap thoughts, vain imaginings and egotistical desires which I saw whenever I directed my attention inwards, then it was a very tawdry affair, so loosely strung together and so dependent on the outer world as to be completely unworthy of surviving when its habitat, the body, crumbled away. Of the self which Berkeley had spoken, the self that was known intuitively, I had as yet no experience. If it were hidden under all that litter of rubbish, then it was undoubtedly very well hidden. But was it actually there or had the theologians and the poets invented it? I could not be sure.

Ouspensky was very late in appearing that night, but it was clear that he was somewhere in the building, for every now and then his secretary entered the room to summon someone out of it. Meanwhile the rest of us sat on in a silence that was broken only by an occasional shuffling of feet, or by an attempt on someone's part to find a more comfortable position on his hard chair. When eventually the lecturer did appear, he immediately began to talk on the subject he had discussed at the previous meeting – man's lack of inner unity. 'Man,' he began, 'is not one person, but many people. He has not one mind, but many minds, a different mind, indeed, for each variety of function. One mind or centre – either name will do – controls his thinking, another deals with his emotions, another with his life of movement and a fourth with all the physiological processes of his body, digestion, respiration, metabolism and activities of that sort. We will call this last mind the instinctive centre. This means that our machinery is regulated by four principal centres in us, the intellectual, the emotional, the moving and the instinctive. It is important to be absolutely clear about these centres and the only way to understand them is to watch them working in ourselves. Observe yourselves and find your own examples of the working of the four centres. There is yet another one – the sex centre – but if you learn about the other centres first you will learn a great deal about the sex centre.'

He then went on to say that there was some overlapping in the activities of these centres and that one centre often took on the work of another one. He gave as an example of this what happened in the process of learning to carry out a number of complicated movements, such as was entailed in acquiring the art of riding a bicycle, playing the piano, or using a typewriter. At the start everything depended on the intellectual centre. One had to think all the time how to distribute one's balance and in what direction to turn the front wheel of the bicycle. One had to look for the right note on the keyboard of the piano, or the right letter on the typewriter. Intellectual centre was so engrossed in all this work that it could think of nothing else, and if someone asked a question at this stage of the lessons, everything immediately went wrong and one had to start again from the beginning. But if one persevered there eventually came a stage in the learning when the necessary movements were performed so easily that there was no longer need to think. It was as though some other part of oneself had taken over the work, had freed the intellectual centre of its duties and had thus allowed it to think. This was exactly what had happened – moving centre was now discharging the duties for which intellectual centre had previously been responsible. This stage at which one centre took over the work of another often began so suddenly that one could name the hour when the change occurred.

Ouspensky's classification of human functions greatly interested me. I had never been really satisfied with the catalogue of psychological functions to be found in modern text-books of psychology, and Ouspensky's divisions had much to commend them. I could also readily accept the idea that thinking, feeling and moving were controlled by different minds, or centres, even although it was difficult to regard the physiological processes of the body as being regulated by a mind. Hormones played a large part in coordinating the activities of bodily organs, but it was true that the output of these hormones was governed by the central nervous system. Physiologists of course were committed to explaining the working of the body purely in terms of the physico-chemical processes, for like other scientists, they had accepted the machine as their working model. But could any machinery, however elaborate it was, do what our living bodies managed to do? I very much doubted it and I was quite prepared to accept, purely as a tentative theory, the idea that all physiological processes were controlled by a centre, or 'intelligence'. It would be situated no doubt in the medulla oblongata and in the sympathetic plexuses. Ouspensky's theory that there was a corresponding intelligence for movements presented no difficulties to me. How otherwise than by the possession of a moving centre could the complicated movements and adjustments made by birds in their flight be explained? Physiologists would probably agree that there were coordinating 'centres' for movements and would refer one to the motor area of the cerebral hemispheres and the cerebellum.

Mr Ouspensky went on with his description of the centres. He said that when moving centre had learnt its job and had taken over the control of movements, it discharged it with far greater efficiency than the intellectual centre had previously done. If intellectual centre attempted to do what moving centre now did, efficiency of movement was reduced. If, for example, the pianist deliberately searched for the notes on the keyboard, or the typist thought of the position of each letter on his typewriter, work was immediately slowed down. He said that this was due to the different speeds at which the various centres worked. Intellectual centre worked at a much lower speed than did the moving and emotional centres, and he gave figures representing the rates between the speeds of these different 'minds'. These figures had not been obtained directly by observation, but indirectly from other data. The fact that instinctive centre – the centre controlling the inner working of the body – functioned at a speed far exceeding the speed of thought explained what was otherwise inexplicable. 'Think,' he said, 'of the many things that happen when a man swallows a glass of brandy. Within a few seconds he becomes conscious of a great many changes in himself, of a warm glow in the region of his stomach, of a flushed face, of a speeding up of his heart, of a different attitude to the world in general and of a feeling of well-being. An immense number of processes have had to be gone through in order that these changes may be brought about. The brandy has had to be absorbed through the walls of the stomach, carried in the bloodstream to the liver, submitted to that organ's chemical investigation, passed on, transported to the central nervous system, where other elaborate physico-chemical processes are carried out, processes that culminate in widespread changes throughout the body. A chemical laboratory could perhaps complete all this work in a week, and yet the body manages to do it within a few seconds. 'At first sight,' he said, 'this seems miraculous, but if we keep in mind two things, that time for the cosmos of the cell is different from time as we are familiar with it, and that instinctive centre works at a very high speed, it need no longer surprise us.'

Somebody asked where these centres were. He replied that strictly speaking they extended throughout the whole body, but that the centre of gravity of the intellectual centre lay in the brain and that of the moving centre in the spinal cord. The headquarters of emotional centre might be looked upon as being the solar plexus. 'I am quite aware,' he said, 'that modern science emphasizes the connection between the great basal nuclei of the brain and the expression of the emotions, but in ancient teaching the numerous nerve plexuses scattered throughout the body, and more especially the great plexus that lies below the diaphragm, the solar plexus, have always been considered to be the seat of the emotions. But I would advise you, for the present, to think of these divisions of man in terms of functions rather than of anatomical structures, and they should be studied as such.'

He then developed the idea of these controlling centres, or minds, further by subdividing them into two halves, the positive half and the negative half. In the intellectual centre these took the form of an affirming half and a denying half; they stated that a thing was so, or that it was not so. He said that in moving centre the division into negative and positive was only a philosophical one, but that in instinctive centre the two halves dealt with pleasing sensations and with painful ones respectively. I was surprised that he had not given us as an example of the division of instinctive centre into two opposing halves the antithesis between vaso-constrictor and vaso-dilator nerves, between the inhibiting and the accelerator nerves of the heart and between catabolic and anabolic processes. These seemed to be far better instances of positive and negative action in instinctive centre than the example he had given. But I felt that it would have been a mistake for me to have offered these examples of mine at that moment, for he had not yet completed his account of the subdivision of centres.

He then returned to emotional centre and said that we would probably expect him to connect the positive half of emotional centre with pleasant emotions and the negative half with unpleasant emotions, but actually emotional centre did not possess a negative half. In expressing and in feeling unpleasant emotions we made use of instinctive centre instead. This fact that Nature had not provided emotional centre with a negative part was of great importance, for it clearly meant that unpleasant emotions were not essential to living. Yet in spite of their being unnecessary we spent most of our time immersed in these unpleasant emotions, anger, jealousy, disappointment, regret, irritation and many others. Every day we allowed a vast amount of our precious energy to be wasted in this way, never realizing for one moment that they were entirely unnecessary. We went so far as to cherish these harmful activities of ours, and to invest them with an entirely spurious dignity. Poets and dramatists wove them into poems and plays and artists chose them as favourite subjects for painting. That work of genius, *Hamlet*, was made out of material supplied by man's negative emotions, and *Hamlet* was the most admired of all plays. 'And with what,' asked Mr Ouspensky, 'do our newspapers and films supply us? They give their readers exactly what they want most, reports of murders and of other acts of violence, news of famines in different parts of the world, accounts of fires and other disasters in which men, women and children perish, and descriptions of unhappy, tortured and frustrated people. This was what men and women liked to hear about, and this was what the press supplied.'

'What about fear?' someone asked. 'You did not mention this among the negative emotions, and yet to me it would appear to be the commonest of them all.'

'Quite right,' he answered, 'but there are many kinds of fear, and some kinds may be useful. Now if there is one thing of which we can be sure it is that negative emotions serve no useful purpose. So all fears cannot be bracketed together as negative emotions, for as I have said, there are such things as useful fears. Suppose that you are walking too near the edge of a cliff and that the ground under your feet begins to give. You are swept by a sudden wave of panic and fling yourself on to the ground away from the cliff's edge. An alarm has been sounded in you and you've responded to it far more quickly than thought. This is an example of an instinctive fear, the kind that animals have. A horse will swerve suddenly when trotting through a forest because it has seen, or heard, a snake, even although it has never come across one before. But most of the things we fear never happen and are creations only of our imaginations. We spend our time inventing all sorts of fictitious future disasters for ourselves, losing our health and our means of livelihood, being involved in an accident, anything and everything. These imaginary events produce in us entirely unnecessary anxiety. They give rise to the most pernicious of our negative emotions and sap our energy.'

I would have liked to have stood up and shouted, 'Hear! hear!' for I had long come to the conclusion that chronic anxiety was one of the most potent factors in the causation of disease. It was certainly the symptom which patients displayed most frequently in the consulting-room, so often indeed that I was always on the look-out for it. To my way of thinking anxiety was the chief cause of the increased incidence in the urban population of duodenal ulcer and coronary thrombosis. It was quite impossible to calculate the amount of harm that living in fear inflicted on our minds and bodies. There was no need for Ouspensky to emphasize to me how vast was the quantity of vital energy lost through imaginary fears. No, it was a mistake to call them imaginary fears, for to the victim they were as real as any fear of falling off a cliff. Anxiety about imaginary events was attended by the same outpouring of adrenalin into the circulation and by the same sudden rise of blood-pressure that occurred with the fear of falling off a cliff. As a doctor I was even more aware than Ouspensky of the amount of energy lost through negative imagination.

'What can we do about negative emotions?' asked a lady whose face clearly showed that she had had a long acquaintanceship with fear. 'I'm sure that I don't enjoy them.'

'Don't be too certain about that,' Ouspensky said. 'Some people have nothing else, and if one could relieve them of their negative emotions, their lives would become blanks.'

'I'll take that risk if you will tell me what to do.'

'First, see them and then make a compact with yourself not to express them.'

'Will that get rid of them?'

'No, for that we would have to be able to "do", and as we are now, everything happens in us. Man is a machine and he has no will, but so long as we go on expressing our negative emotions freely, we don't even notice them. First it is necessary to see them.'

'Why?' asked somebody. 'Surely we can take them for granted.'

'Nothing must be taken for granted,' replied Mr Ouspensky firmly. 'Everything I tell you must be tested. Faith is not wanted here. You must know the taste of your negative emotions and recognize one at once as soon as it begins to arise in you. At the very beginning it may be possible to prevent the negative emotion from becoming stronger, but when it has fully developed, you will be completely in its power. So far, I have told you to do one thing only, namely, to observe yourselves, but now I add to this something else – try not to express your negative emotions. Next time report to me your discoveries.'

'I don't see what is to be gained by seeing more of one's negative emotions, if, having seen them, there is nothing to be done about them,' someone objected.

'I did not say that there was nothing to be done about them,' he answered. 'You are in too great a hurry, and with the little material we have at present, it is impossible for me to go further. I will have more to say later after we have discussed such questions as identification, and then you will see that our position is not quite so hopeless as it now appears to be.'

An elderly woman who up till then had asked no questions now spoke in a very quiet voice, so quietly that I had difficulty in hearing her. 'Do you mean to say, Mr Ouspensky, that all sorrow is entirely useless and even pernicious? If one loses somebody who is very dear to one ...'

He interrupted her. 'There is sorrow and there is sorrow. All suffering is not negative emotion. One may learn from suffering but from negative emotion one learns nothing. But suffering may turn into negative emotion unless one is very careful. I take the example you have given. One loses a near relation or a friend and experiences genuine sorrow, but in the course of time a healthy person recovers from this. The loss is still there but he no longer broods over it. But it is very easy to graft on to the original sorrow a negative attitude to everything in life, to become for ever irreconcilable to the loss. That is what I mean by saying that suffering may turn into a negative emotion.' She thanked him for his answer in the same quiet voice and Ouspensky then asked if there were any more questions. After waiting a minute or two he went out of the room.

I had been on the point of speaking about emotions, but I had had difficulty in finding the right words. Now it was too late and I regretted that I had lost my opportunity of asking questions, not only about negative emotions, but also about the psychological divisions he had made. The idea of the four centres greatly interested me. I wondered if it was an Eastern method of classification and I recalled that Jung had said that Westerners were as children in comparison with Easterners so far as a knowledge of psychology was concerned. M. had long ago described the system of knowledge that Ouspensky taught as an Eastern system presented in a form suited to the Western mind. I wanted to know a great deal more about it and also to find out the real reason for holding these meetings. But it would be better, I thought, to put these questions to Ouspensky in private. Why should I not ask for a private interview with him? It was obvious that other people were seeing him in the little room at the end of the passage, and I had the same right as they to take up a little of his time.

On my way out I spoke to the Russian lady in the hall and asked her whether it would be possible for me to have a few words with Mr Ouspensky. 'If you will wait a moment or two I'll find out whether he can see you.' She returned soon with the message that Mr Ouspensky was fully occupied at present, but that if I cared to go to 228 Gwendyr Road at five o'clock on Thursday he would be pleased to see me there. This appointment was very suitable and having found out where Gwendyr Road was, I left the building.

I felt that there was something reassuring about Mr Ouspensky's method of teaching, and any suspicions with which I had arrived at his meeting, two weeks previously, had by now completely disappeared. What I liked most was that he made no attempt to foist his ideas on to his hearers, but contented himself with formulating them as clearly as possible and then leaving it to his audience to accept these ideas or not. But how wrong I had been in believing that the people who attended these meetings did so only in the hope of finding soothing doctrines which would render their lives more tolerable to them. So far, he had spent his time shattering the few illusions that modern people still retained and giving them little or nothing to put in their place. No, this was not quite true, for tonight he had suggested that there were methods of dealing with negative emotions and possibilities of avoiding the wastage of energy that they caused. If he could teach us how to do that I would be able to understand why people continued to come to his meetings. Nor was he so coldly philosophical and intellectual as I had at first thought, for he had answered that woman with the quiet voice more emotionally than I had expected. She had obviously known true sorrow and he knew that she was still suffering from some great personal loss.

CHAPTER III

A TALK WITH OUSPENSKY

THE architecture of Gwendyr Road is late Victorian and the houses that line it are uniformly dismal in pattern. They were evidently run up at great speed and at a minimum cost at a time when London was rapidly expanding to meet the needs of the industrial age. On one side of each dwelling is placed a front door with four stone steps leading up to it, and on the other a bow-window. The houses have an air of smug respectability, but they are now beginning to look a little forlorn, as though they were finding it more and more difficult to retain their primness in a new and disconcerting world. How incongruous it seemed that I should be seeking for the abode of an exponent of Eastern wisdom in such an unmistakably British street as this.

I rang the bell of No. 228 and as there was no answer peered through the stained-glass panel of the front door. It was opened at last by a woman who could only be a landlady and I was shown into a room on the first floor. She told me that Mr Ouspensky was in, but that he was busy in the basement developing photographs. Would I please take a seat.

Why should it be thought that the thing a person who is being kept waiting needs most is a seat? I had no desire for a seat, and had no intention of sitting down, for I was far more interested in the room in which Mr Ouspensky fed, slept, wrote and thought than in planting myself on a chair. To my mind a man's room is far more revealing than are the clothes he wears, and I welcomed this opportunity of prowling about in Ouspensky's lair. Along one wall was a bed and opposite it were two comfortable chairs on each side of a gas-fire. Another wall was taken up by a low bookcase and in the centre of the room there stood a large square mahogany table. On this rested a heap of sundries, books, papers, a typewriter, photographs, coloured reproductions of the work of some of the Old Masters, writing materials, letters, a camera, a galvanometer and a piece of some scientific instrument of the nature of which I was uncertain. On the mantelpiece there was a half-finished tin of sardines, the remains of a loaf, a plate with its knife and fork, crumbs and a fragment of cheese. Evidently he had recently eaten standing by the mantelpiece, probably because the table was already too cluttered with things to be used – a most sensible arrangement of which I fully approved. It showed that he had a nice disregard for the inconveniences of which life is chiefly composed and that he possessed a sense of proportion. Now I would study the titles of some of his books, and first, of those lying open before me on the table. But as I was on the point of beginning my literary investigation I heard footsteps approaching on the stairs and I quickly did what I was supposed to have done long before – I sat down.

He entered the room and, as I rose to greet him, apologized for having kept me waiting, explaining that there were some plates that had to be fixed and washed, as otherwise they would have been spoilt. Would I please sit down, and as it was cold in here he would light the gas-fire. We both sat down and looked at the flames colouring the asbestos, at first a faint rose and then later a brilliant red. After a long pause Mr Ouspensky turned to me and uttered the word with which he introduced all discussions, the solitary word, 'Well?' It was the signal to begin and I began by telling him how interested I was in his lectures. I said that the ideas that I had heard seemed to me to be of great psychological importance and that I had been particularly impressed by his classification of man's functions and by his conception of the existence of different minds, or controlling centres. He nodded and waited for me to continue. 'I have never been satisfied with the divisions used by McDougall, or Freud, or Jung. Freud has the idea that in his hands psychology has become a science, but —'

Mr Ouspensky interrupted me. 'So far we have been dealing not with psychology, but with mechanics,' he said. 'Psychology applies to *men* only, and up till now we have been considering only the man-machine. Psychology will come later when we talk about real men.'

I did not want to discuss with him the idea that man was an automaton at that moment, so I made no comment. I was quite prepared to admit that most of our actions were reflex actions, but I was not yet convinced that we were so devoid of will as

Ouspensky maintained. In any case I preferred to talk about something else. 'May I ask you a question?' I said.

'Certainly.'

'Why are you giving these lectures, Mr Ouspensky? What is your motive? Is it philanthropy?'

He laughed and shook his head.

'Is this because in teaching others one clarifies one's own ideas? As you probably know, I am on the teaching staff of St Bartholomew's Hospital and I find that teaching others is a great help to thought.'

'Perhaps partly,' he answered.

'I notice,' I continued, 'that you have people in your audience who belong to a number of different professions, scientists, doctors, architects, artists and so on. Do you get some advantage from their expert knowledge, say, in the developing of your own ideas?'

'Maybe,' he answered, after a pause. 'But there are other reasons besides these,' he added. 'You may discover what they are later.' Having said this he relapsed into silence and we again stared at the fire.

'What is the aim of this system of knowledge?' I asked. 'I mean by this, what is the aim of this thing that people at your meetings call the work?'

'The system itself has no aim and cannot have an aim, but those who want to acquire this knowledge must have an aim. You must know your own aim if you are to get any benefit from coming to my meetings,'

'Why?'

'Well, you may discover that what you get at my meetings does not help your aim, or else you may find that it does. It will be impossible for you to decide whether it is the right thing for you unless you know clearly where you want to go. To have a clearly defined aim in life – and few people have – is of the greatest importance. This is the meaning of some of the old fairy stories, and fairy stories often have hidden meanings. For example, there is the common story about a fairy or a genie, who appears and offers to grant the wish of the chief character. The story then goes on to narrate how the recipient of the offer does not know which gift to choose, or else he chooses so unwisely that when he has been granted three wishes – as so often happens in this kind of story – the last has to be used up in getting rid of what he had previously received. When the recipient has chosen the wrong thing and has been granted only one wish, then his mistake may kill him, as was the case with Midas.'

These words of Mr Ouspensky about the need for knowing what one wanted reminded me of something else. This would be a good opportunity for letting him know something about myself. 'You have a very mixed audience,' I began, 'but if you were to ask me what these people had in common, I would say that it was disillusionment with life. They come to you because they are disappointed and want to discover a philosophy of living. Now I would like you to know that this does not apply to me. I'm a confirmed optimist and I find life more and more satisfactory. I come to you because I happen to be interested in your ideas, and I can assure you that I'm quite contented with things as they are. I have excellent health. I have no financial or private worries and I thoroughly enjoy my work.'

As I have previously pointed out, Mr Ouspensky's most striking quality was his solidity and his serenity, and I could see that he had not been in the least impressed by this catalogue of personal assets. His expression showed no change, and I had the feeling that it would not have altered even if I had been able to say: 'I've just been elected President of the Royal College of Surgeons and, last week, I rode my own mount in the Grand National and won it ...' He evidently had his own yardstick with which to measure success in life and it was now apparent that his yardstick was not the same as mine. For a time there was silence, and then he said: 'There is far less difference than you think between the man who says that life is not worth living and the one who believes that everything in it is splendid. Let me see, I think it was through M. that you came to Warwick Gardens?'

'Yes, he's a very old friend of mine.'

'I understand both you and him, because there were two friends very similar in our Moscow group. You two and they belong to the same two types, only you happen to be a successful representative of your type and the other man who corresponded to you wasn't. The study of types is a very interesting one.'

It was gratifying to know that one was a successful representative of a type, but I would have preferred to have been accepted by Mr

Ouspensky as an individual instead of being allotted to a group. How impersonal he was, and how difficult it had suddenly become to begin an intimate conversation with a man who remained so far away from one as he did. I felt that the enthusiasm with which I had entered the room was ebbing out of me and after making a few general remarks of no interest to either of us, I rose to go. The interview had ended in disappointment and nothing had been achieved. I admired this man but it seemed that we were to meet always as strangers.

Mr Ouspensky had excellent manners, and, having accompanied me to the door, he remained there till I had driven away. I regretted now that I had brought the conversation round to myself. It would have been much better to have discussed only generalities. How difficult it was to talk to a man who answered questions but who never initiated any conversation himself. Although he was only five or six years my senior, I felt very much as I had been accustomed to feel at school when, as a prefect, I had been called into the headmaster's room for a friendly talk. Nominally I had permission to discuss anything I liked, but I was always too conscious of the difference between myself and the headmaster to be able to converse with any sense of freedom.

If my private talk with Mr Ouspensky had been a failure, the next meeting at Warwick Gardens was the very reverse of this. It was certainly the most interesting meeting I had attended, and it left the deepest impression on me that had yet been made. The subject of consciousness was discussed and Mr Ouspensky started by warning us not to confuse consciousness with thought. 'Consciousness,' he said, 'could not be defined, but everybody knew what it was.' Thinking, feeling, sensing and moving were functions and consciousness was awareness of these functions. It was a subjective state that could only be known by experiencing it. There were four possible states of it, namely, sleep and the condition in which we spent our days, a condition that we would call waking sleep. It was generally said that man was a self-conscious being, but this statement was quite untrue. Man was only very rarely aware of himself, and he spent almost the whole of his time in a state that differed very little from that in which he passed his nights. It was for this reason that he had described man's state as one of waking sleep. He then asked us all to make an experiment.

'Look at a watch,' he said, 'and try to be aware of yourself all the time you are looking at it. Say to yourself, "I am looking at this watch," and make an effort to feel yourself sitting there, gazing at your watch and following the second hand as it moves round. All the time keep up the feeling of "I", maintain your awareness of your existence there in that room, and see how long you are able to continue doing this. You'll find that you will not manage to maintain self-consciousness for more than about two minutes, and if you repeat the experiment soon afterwards, it will not last even as long as this. By making these experiments you will learn what self-consciousness really means, and for what a short time it lasts. I find it useful to represent to myself this state of self-consciousness diagrammatically by a double-headed arrow.' He walked over to the blackboard and drew a tiny cross on it. 'This,' he said, 'represents a man and this line going out from him with an arrowhead on the end of it represents the line of his attention. He is looking at a lamp-post and he is aware of the lamp-post alone. This second diagram that I draw now represents a man who is looking at the lamp-post and at the same time trying to self-remember, that is to say, to be aware of himself. Here I draw on the line two arrow-heads, one pointing to the lamp-post and the other pointing back to the man. The two arrowheads indicate that his attention is divided so that he is aware, not only of the lamp-post, but also of himself looking at the lamp-post. It is essential that you should understand this, for it is one of the most important ideas in this system. If you have any doubt about it, please ask questions.'

'I don't see how a person can self-remember if he hasn't got a "self" to remember,' objected someone. 'You said at another meeting that a man had no self, but only a lot of changing "I"s.' The speaker was a young man whom I had noticed before because he formulated his questions so clearly. The exactitude with which he spoke convinced me that he was either a lawyer or a schoolmaster.

'Don't confuse yourself with words but think only of ideas. Don't bother about having a permanent "I" or not having a permanent "I". Just try to become aware of your existence, of your body, to begin with. Try to realize that you are here, at this moment of time, sitting in a chair in this very room with your knees crossed, waiting for my answer. I speak of something very practical and not of theories about having a self or not having a self. Make experiments, not now, but when you return home. After you have made them, bring your observations here and ask any questions you like.'

As there were no more questions on the subject of self-remembering Mr Ouspensky continued his discussion of states of consciousness. 'I have told you,' he said, 'that you must make a special effort to create self-awareness for yourselves, but sometimes it happens spontaneously without any effort, especially in childhood. When people look back on their lives many of them recall moments when they seemed to come out of a daze and to become acutely aware of themselves. At such moments they were acutely conscious of their existence, of their standing apart from all that surrounded them. They experienced that strong feeling of "I" that consciousness always brings with it, "I" and all the rest that is not "I". I said that this happens more frequently in childhood but it may happen in adult life, especially in moments of personal danger, or when one is travelling in a strange and unfamiliar country. These are very vivid moments, and because of this they are generally remembered for the whole of one's life. Indeed, it may be said that the only moments that a person really remembers are these moments in which he becomes aware of himself. And by remember I don't mean simply that he is able to tell you that such and such a thing happened to him but that he can bring back to himself the whole scene, all his surroundings at that time, how he felt, what he thought, everything. It all comes back to him, exactly as it was.'

I was too absorbed in what Mr Ouspensky was saying to want to ask questions. Here was somebody explaining to me something that had always puzzled me and about which nobody had ever been able to tell me anything – those startling moments in childhood in which I had 'come to'. It was just like emerging from an anaesthetic and finding oneself in a dentist's chair, or lying in bed, and 'coming to' were the words that I had always used when describing these experiences to myself. There was the same sudden realization of being there, with that abrupt influx of impressions coming in from outside. At those moments sounds of which one had previously been unaware began to flow in, colours became more vivid and everything outside one, as well as everything within one, came to life. The change was so startling that one stopped whatever one was doing at the time and waited expectantly for some other miracle to happen. If this was what Mr Ouspensky meant by self-consciousness, then certainly one spent practically the whole of the rest of one's life in an entirely different state, asleep, dwelling in a kind of perpetual twilight, like fishes at the bottom of the sea. Although I had never explained these moments satisfactorily to myself as Mr Ouspensky had just done, I had somehow realized that if I wanted to taste life more fully, I must struggle upwards towards the surface of that sea where there was more light. I recalled a time in Africa, when I was shooting, many years ago. My companion and I had been following elephant all day, and just when we were getting near to them darkness had fallen, so that we were forced to encamp. As I lay in my camp-bed that night listening to trumpetings and to the breaking of branches in the nearby forest, I kept repeating to myself the words, 'I am here, I, who am listening to great wild elephants, not just tame ones, feeding only a few hundred yards from me. I am actually here in this tent and I am listening to elephants.' And this emphasis on 'I' increased the vividness of everything so that I had more pleasure in it. But I must not think about this now. I must pay attention to what Ouspensky was saying in case I should lose something of great importance.

'Above true self-consciousness,' he said, 'there lie two higher states of which we know nothing, although descriptions of them may be found in literature. Usually these higher states are described in books as though they were only one state, under such a heading as "objective consciousness", or "cosmic consciousness". In them a man makes connection with two other centres that I have not yet described, called "higher emotional centre" and "higher intellectual centre". These centres exist in us already formed, but intellectual centre works so slowly and these higher centres so quickly, that no connection can be made between them. We are therefore unaware of their existence. It is like having a powerful arc-lamp in the house of which no use can be made because it is not yet properly connected up with the electric circuit. But just as an ordinary sleeping man can occasionally experience brief moments of self-consciousness, so can a man who has attained self-consciousness occasionally have glimpses of these higher states. These glimpses can also be obtained artificially by the use of certain drugs, such as hashish. If you are interested in them you can find descriptions of them in many books, and more particularly in works dealing with the lives of the saints. But you won't learn much from reading them, for language was made for everyday life; it provides no words by which things so far removed from ordinary existence can be described. Even if a special language were to be invented by those who have had experience of higher states of consciousness, this language would not be of much use, for the real languages of higher emotional and higher intellectual centres are the languages of allegory and symbol respectively. It is by these means that their truths can best be transmitted and later we may study a symbol in which many truths are so embodied. But I warn you that you will only be able to comprehend a few of these truths.'

'Symbolism is much used in art,' said a lady in a hand-woven dress. Her smooth, dark hair was drawn tightly back across her temples and she wore shoes resembling sandals. 'Would you say, Mr Ouspensky, that symbolic art was the product of the working of some higher centre?'

'There are different levels of art,' he replied, 'just as there are different levels of men, but symbolism in ordinary art – the art that we know – is the product of the artist's dreams. In much of modern art it is the product of his nightmares. Such art is purely subjective and means nothing at all. Any more questions?'

Somebody suggested that Freud had made valuable contributions to this idea of different levels of consciousness. He had described three levels, the unconscious, the pre-conscious and the conscious.

'Freud came near to many things,' answered Mr Ouspensky. 'But just as he seems to be on the point of making an important discovery, he suddenly sheers off in another direction. It is surprising that having got so far, he was unable to get further. But what is the good of talking about consciousness when a man does not possess it?'

I was not fully satisfied with his answer. I felt that although it was true that Freud had failed to recognize that man was not really self-conscious, he had nevertheless made an important contribution to psychology by directing attention to levels of consciousness below the level at which we habitually lived. His chief error was his failure to realize that there might exist states of consciousness as far above the ordinary level as the subconscious was below it.

'Consciousness may be likened to light,' continued Ouspensky after he had answered several other questions. 'Imagine a room in which there are several machines working. One of these machines is intellectual centre, another emotional centre and a third moving centre. These machines can work in the dark, but if candles are lit they work better. By installing electric light in the workshop they work still more efficiently, and when the blinds are drawn up and sunlight enters through the windows, they are at their best. Compare our intelligence, as measured by our ability to adjust ourselves to our environment, when we are in bed at night, with our intelligence in the state of waking sleep. While we are asleep in bed impressions still continue to reach us, noises from the street, sensations of heat and cold and a sense of the weight of the bedclothes. These messages from the outside world provoke reactions which are often revealed in our dreams. We try to move our feet, entangled perhaps in the sheet, discover that we cannot do this, and then dream that we are stuck fast in a bog, and that some horrible creature is pursuing us. In other words, our interpretation of the messages that reach us from outside is an entirely subjective interpretation which bears little or no relationship to reality. When we get out of bed our interpretation of sensory messages is more realistic, and as a result we are able to orientate ourselves much better to changes in our environment. We can, for example, see danger ahead, and can take steps to avoid it. But if we consider things a little more carefully we shall see that potentially we are in an even more dangerous position during waking sleep than when we are in bed. In this waking state one "I" in us may do something foolish for which all the other "I"s in us may afterwards be compelled to pay. In bed we were passive and were called upon to make no vital decisions, but out of it we can decide to do things that may have exceedingly harmful results, not only for ourselves, but for everybody else. One "I" may sign a promissory note for which the whole of us will afterwards become

43

responsible. It must be remembered that we do not see the real world as it actually is, but only the world that our imaginations have painted for us. If we could become self-conscious we would see things more as they are. Life would then assume an entirely different aspect and it would acquire a new meaning for us. In that higher state of consciousness in which higher emotional centre works, a man becomes objective to himself; in the highest state of all, with the higher intellectual centre working, he sees not only himself but the whole universe as it actually is. But we will not talk about these highest states for they are too far away from us. Instead, we will talk only about what is practical for us, namely, the transitional state of self-consciousness.'

'Is that why you said self-remembering was so important?' asked someone.

He nodded. 'To try to self-remember is to try to stir in your sleep. It is an effort to awaken and become self-conscious.'

'But if one is going about all day thinking about oneself, won't it —?'

Mr Ouspensky interrupted him. 'Self-remembering is not thinking,' he said, 'it is consciousness, awareness of oneself and of all that is happening both within and without. There can be thinking without consciousness and there is such a thing as consciousness without thought. Try to understand what I am saying.'

'But if,' continued the same questioner, 'one were to go about all day remembering oneself, wouldn't —?'

Mr Ouspensky again stopped him. 'Can you do this? Can you remain all the time self-conscious? Go and do this, and when you have succeeded, come back here and put to me the question you wanted to ask. I'll answer you then.' He turned to other members of his audience. 'We'll speak of this again,' he said, 'but not until you have more material in the way of self-observations. This idea of self-remembering is not just a theory; it is something that can, and should, be put into practice. It is very important, perhaps the most important thing that I have to tell you.' Having said this he left the room abruptly.

As I drove back to Harley Street I went over in my mind all that Ouspensky had said, and thought particularly about his statement that men lived in a state of sleep, that they were only at rare moments aware of themselves. Here was something that could not be just blindly accepted but must be submitted to a personal test. I would make this experiment that he had suggested with a watch and I would try to observe the minor fluctuations of consciousness that occurred throughout the day. If it were really true that men were asleep, what a revolutionary change would be required in our views of human life on this planet. A sleeping world – people walking in the street, sitting in government offices, conducting the affairs of the state, hurrying into the lobby of the Houses of Parliament to record their votes, dispensing justice from the bench, doing a thousand different things, and all of these activities carried out in sleep! Ouspensky could not have meant that. Yes, he *had* meant that and he had either been talking arrant nonsense or else making the most startling statement that it was possible for any person to make. A sleepwalker's world, a world inhabited by people who moved about in a twilight of consciousness and yet imagined that they were fully awake. What situation could be more dangerous than this, or lead to greater misunderstanding amongst men? Well, if lack of understanding was regarded as a proof of the accuracy of Ouspensky's statement, there was no difficulty in supplying it. Nobody seemed to be able to understand anybody else in this world of ours. It was a world of absurdities, of nations offering friendship and at the same time preparing for war, of people saying one thing and doing another, of walking in circles, of paper plans and of general chaos. All this would be easily explained if it were true that we were all asleep, but for the present I would neither accept nor reject this astounding theory. I would let it lie on the table of my mind and carry out the experiment which Ouspensky had suggested. I would test my own self-awareness by means of what he called 'self-remembering' and discover whether I was awake or asleep.

CHAPTER IV

ESOTERIC KNOWLEDGE

LOOKING back as I now do I clearly see that the meeting
described in the previous chapter marked a critical point in the
journey of which this book is a chronicle. Hitherto I had been
interested in much that I heard at Warwick Gardens, but no more
than I would have been in some book which I had accidentally
come across and started to read. I had felt that it was well worth
my while making the weekly journey to Warwick Gardens provided
that I had no more important engagement on that evening. If
somebody had asked me my opinion of Mr Ouspensky's lectures I
would have replied that he had many original ideas and that his
views on psychology were particularly interesting. But from now
onwards my attitude to him and to what he taught began to
change. Not only did the meetings become of far greater importance to me but I examined everything I heard there with much
greater care. Many of Ouspensky's statements could not be
proved, but there were others that could be put to a practical test.
Whenever I did this with a psychological idea, I found it to be
true. For example, I now realized exactly what Ouspensky meant
when he said that man was not aware of himself and that he spent
his waking hours in a condition that differs very little from sleep.
It was ridiculous to call the state in which we spend practically the
whole of the day self-consciousness. We fumble through life
completely unaware of what we are doing and responding in a
dull-witted way to external stimuli. To be conscious, say the
dictionaries, is to have one's faculties awake, but how often are we
able to claim that our faculties are awake? Perhaps only for a
moment during the course of the whole day. For the rest of the
time visual impressions flood in through the eyes, but there is no
one there to record them. Sounds impinge on the ears and rever-
berate through the rooms of an empty house. The owner is not at
home because he lives elsewhere in a world of dreams. I had also
followed Mr Ouspensky's instructions and had made efforts to

self-remember, but with very little success. It was startling and humiliating to find how quickly this intentionally induced state of self-awareness came to an end however hard one struggled to maintain it. I had also tested his machine-theory by trying to do things in some different way – to behave differently, for example, when in the company of someone I disliked – and had found that it was quite impossible for me to do this. These discoveries were disconcerting, but they increased my confidence in Mr Ouspensky and in the ideas of the system.

It was, perhaps, as well that this confidence had grown. I found the next few meetings less interesting than the previous ones. Instead of continuing his description of man, he began to talk of the universe in which man lived. It was useless, he said, to study things in a state of isolation; they must be studied in their surroundings, for everything in the universe was affected by everything else. If therefore we were to discover more about man, we must also investigate the universe in which man lived. It was just about this time that I discovered A. N. Whitehead, and as his philosophy of organism was becoming more and more important to me, I readily accepted Ouspensky's statement that things must always be studied in their setting because it was completely in harmony with Whitehead's views. Ouspensky then went on to say that man was a miniature of the universe in which he lived and that everything in him, as in it, was controlled by the same two great cosmic laws, the Law of Three and the Law of Seven. This, he said, was the meaning of the ancient saying that man was a 'microcosm in a macrocosm'. It also explained that other ancient dictum, 'As above, so below.' He then described the two great cosmic laws which determined the whole process of world creation. The law of three postulated that all phenomena of every possible kind were the result of the interaction of three forces which could be called either first, second and third force, or else active force, passive force and neutralizing force. Science sometimes recognized the existence of two forces in a phenomenon, for example, positive and negative electricity, but it had no knowledge of a third force. Yet without the intervention of a third force nothing could be brought into being. In ordinary states of consciousness we could be said to be 'third force blind', but in spite of this we must try to find examples of three forces interacting to produce a phenomenon.

At this point a man with stubborn coarse hair which, in spite of a liberal supply of brilliantine, insisted on standing up on end like the bristles of a scrubbing-brush, asked for an example of the action of a third force.

'You must find your own examples,' answered Ouspensky. 'Some people,' he added after a short pause, 'find it easier to discover psychological examples from self-observation and others may more readily see the action of a third force in the world without. The catalytic agent in chemistry may be looked upon as being a third force.'

The stubborn-looking man – his character was certainly in keeping with his hair – did not appear to be completely satisfied and there was silence in the room. Ouspensky was evidently waiting for us to find our own examples of the law of three, but it was difficult to find illustrations of an idea that was so novel as this. I thought of several instances in endocrinology where two ductless glands acted on an organ to produce some change in it, and I wondered whether this was an example of three forces. As nobody had anything to offer him, Mr Ouspensky turned from the law of three to the other great cosmic law, the law of seven.

He said that another name for it was the law of octaves. It showed the process of development of phenomena in time and would be well illustrated by the study of the creation of new worlds. Tonight, he said, we would look upon the universe as being made up of energy or of vibrations proceeding in all directions, crossing one another, colliding with one another and reinforcing one another. Western science often regarded the universe from the standpoint of vibrations, as he was going to do, but science did not understand that these vibrations did not develop uninterruptedly. They were subject to interruptions, and ancient knowledge realized this and laid emphasis on the discontinuity of the development of vibrations. At certain points there occurred a retardation of the development of vibrations, and this knowledge had obviously been known to those who had originated the seven-tone musical scale. The seven-tone scale might indeed be looked upon as being a formula of the great cosmic law of seven applied to music by those who belonged to some ancient esoteric school. At two place in the scale, namely, between the notes mi and fa and between the notes si and do, a semitone was missing. It was at these points in an ascending octave that the rate of the increase of vibrations slowed down, or in a descending octave that their rate of retardation diminished. These points would in future be referred to as the intervals in the octave. 'And,' continued Ouspensky, 'it is at the intervals, or where the increase or decrease of the frequency of vibrations is retarded that an octave is likely to proceed no further. It is then also that it often changes its direction. We have many instances of this happening in our private activities. Suppose, for example, we start to learn something, such as a new language, and sound the doh for the new octave. For a time all goes well, but a little later on we come to a very difficult period when perhaps our initial enthusiasm has evaporated and we encounter unexpected obstacles. It is here that the octave we have started is likely to stop, or to change in some way. Only if some other octave coming from somewhere else strikes across this interval and, as it were, fills the gap and thereby reinforces the original impetus, do we manage to continue.

He then proceeded to draw on the blackboard a diagram that he called the Ray of Creation. This showed the development of 'worlds' in accordance with the working of the two great cosmic laws, starting with the Absolute and coming down to our earth through the various stages of the great stellar galaxies, the sun, the planetary worlds, the earth and beyond us the moon. After having explained to us the diagram in greater detail, he pointed out that it represented the universe as being still in the process of creation. It was not, as science represented it, something that had been brought into being and then left to run down slowly, but something that was still in the process of making itself. Instead of the sun growing colder, it was becoming hotter and hotter, and instead of the moon being a dead frozen world, it was a small world that had not yet reached its full development. It would be better therefore for us to look upon the universe as a living organism throwing out new branches and growing new shoots and not as a clock that had once been wound up and was now running down. Mr Ouspensky resumed his seat and invited questions.

'What about the second law of thermodynamics?' asked the man with the scrubbing-brush hair. 'This idea that the universe is still evolving is quite contrary to the law of increasing entropy.'

'The second law of thermodynamics,' replied Ouspensky, 'is a scientific theory, and scientific theories often have to be abandoned when they no longer serve us.'

'It is the basis of all science,' he protested.

'Even foundations may sometimes prove unsatisfactory and have to be refashioned,' answered Ouspensky with a smile.

The wearer of the tweed coat and the scrubbing-brush hair opened his mouth as though he were about to say something more and then closed it again. Instead of speaking to Mr Ouspensky, he said something in an undertone to his neighbour and then he turned his eyes earthward and contemplated his boots. It was plain that he had lost all interest in anything more that Mr Ouspensky had to say, for what reliance could be placed on the statements of a man who played fast and loose with the second law of thermodynamics!

Mr Ouspensky continued his lecture undisturbed by the havoc he had wrought in the mind of one of his audience. To my delight he returned unexpectedly from the benumbing vastness of space and his examination of evolving worlds to something much nearer home and of far greater importance to me, namely, the significance of man in this immense scheme of creation. 'Individual man,' he began, 'is so small that he cannot be said to exist in the scale of things we have been studying. He exists only as a constituent of organic life, as a tiny part of that thin film of living creatures that covers the surface of the earth. Now, when you look upon the ray of creation as an octave, you will notice that organic life is situated at a very significant place in it. It is situated in the interval that exists between the planetary world and the earth, in other words, just where the diminution in the frequency of the vibrations travelling down the ray is being retarded. Here some outside shock is required to allow these vibrations to pass from the planetary world to the earth, and this necessary shock is provided by the presence there of organic life. The existence of life on this planet is no accident. The film of living creatures spread over the earth plays an important part in the economy of this planet, yes, and in that of the moon also.'

I strained not to miss a word, for here was something that interested me far more than the laws that were to determine world-creations. I had never been able to accept the usual idea that the appearance of life on the earth was the last link in a long chain of accidents. So many favourable conditions had to be provided on the earth before life could exist there that it looked as though special preparations had been made for its advent. Everything suggested that the existence of life on this planet was not fortuitous, but a necessary item in a vast creative plan. I was convinced that for some unknown reason life was necessary to the earth and here was Ouspensky confirming this view. He even gave an account – although an account that it was difficult to accept – of what the function of organic life was. Whether what he was saying was true or not, I could not but admire the bold imaginative sweep of the scheme of creation that he had just laid before us.

'Man serves Nature's purpose as he is, and, so far as the universe is concerned, there is no need for him to change. Asleep or awake, with or without will, a machine or a *man* (he emphasized the last word) he does all that is required of him. If he is to change, if he is to develop his latent powers, it must be for his own purposes and by means of his own individual struggles. Nature has brought his development up to a certain point and has then left him to his own devices. She will help him no more, but she has not denied him the chance of evolving further to a yet higher stage. But if this further evolution is to occur, it will not be by Nature that it is brought about, but by means of man's own conscious struggles. It cannot happen mechanically; will cannot be acquired involuntarily; consciousness cannot be reached in sleep; no accident can change a machine into a man. For this to happen unceasing struggle is necessary, and not only struggle, but knowledge of the way to struggle. But if both of these conditions are satisfied, if a man has knowledge and makes the necessary efforts, he can become something other than he is.' He ended abruptly with these words and waited for questions.

The man with the logical mind, whom I had assumed to be a schoolmaster or lawyer, was the first to speak. 'If, as you tell us, Mr Ouspensky, we are all machines, I do not see how it is possible for us to become anything else. Either we have choice or else we have no choice, and if the latter be true, then how can there be any possibility of change? We are machines and machines we must remain.'

'Look at it this way,' he answered. 'There is what we may call a weak point in our machinery, a place at which we may begin to work, a place where there is less rigidity than elsewhere. You can visualize it as a little give and play between the cog wheels, a freedom that with constant effort may be increased.'

'But surely effort entails will?'

Mr Ouspensky nodded. 'Yes, every time we make a momentary struggle not to react as we have always reacted to something, we are exercising our wills, but unfortunately our efforts only last a very short time. Two minutes later another "I" has appeared and the struggle against mechanicalness immediately ceases. A lasting change can only be brought about by a lifetime of unremitting struggle. In time constant drops of water will wear away something as hard even as a rock.'

'Is it worth it?' exclaimed a woman sitting at the back of the room. So far she had asked no questions and her words seemed to have been uttered against her will.

'That is for you to decide,' he answered promptly. 'If you are content to remain as you are, if you are content to be at the mercy of all chance happenings, then it is certainly not worth your while making all these efforts. But if you have a very strong desire to be free of all this, then it will be different. I advise everybody to think about their aim, for without having an aim nothing can be done. But we will speak about this some other time.' Having said this he made a sign to a stout, rather jovial-looking man with tortoise-shell rimmed glasses, who generally sat near him, to follow him and left the room.

A few minutes later the stout man – I believe he was a doctor – returned and made an announcement. 'Will those who come here in cars,' he said, 'leave them at a garage or at any rate not park them just outside the front door. We don't want to advertise to everybody that meetings are being held here. That's all I've got to say.'

'A lot of nonsense!' murmured the man with the scrubbing-brush hair in my ear.

'You mean all this secrecy?' I answered.

'That amongst other things,' he replied, 'but I was referring to what he calls the ray of creation, all that about the sun and moon getting hotter. It's entirely contrary to scientific knowledge.'

'But I gather that a view is being put forward that the sun may actually be getting hotter by the destruction of atoms!' I hazarded to remark.

'Yes, I know,' he answered, 'but you can't get away from the fact that the second law of thermodynamics is the basis of all modern science. Eddington has said that a crusade against this law is doomed to failure, and it's ridiculous to treat it as though it were of no account. How can one accept anything from a man who does that?'

I bade him a friendly good night and hurried out to my car, that I had fortunately left, not by design but by accident, parked further down the Gardens. The disgruntled scientist's words were still sounding in my ears. 'How can one accept anything from a man who does that?' It would seem that at all costs, and even at the risk of missing some new idea of importance, scientific authority must be upheld. Obviously this man with the obstinate hair would not appear in Warwick Gardens again. He had made conditions for learning anything new and Mr Ouspensky had not observed these. 'What about yourself?' a voice within me asked. Was the second law of thermodynamics sacrosanct for me also? No, but probably something else was. We disliked having the contents of our minds disarranged and undoubtedly many of Ouspensky's ideas could not be accepted without producing at least a temporary state of inner disorder. But I would take warning from this devotee of science and would try to avoid imposing conditions on Ouspensky. Ideas that I could not accept would be put on one side for the time being, and later, when I understood them better, I might be able to fit them into the general pattern of my thought. I would treat in this way his strange notion of organic life being a kind of transmitting apparatus for vibrations reaching the earth from higher levels in the ray of creation. It would be dishonest to pretend that I accepted this at present. Yet Ouspensky had given this idea to us with the same confidence and in the same quiet tone of authority that he used in talking about things that I now knew to be true, such as the idea that man was not really a self-conscious being. There was one more thing I must do and that was to get in touch again with M. and find out from him more about the source of this strange and startling system of knowledge.

On the following week M. and I dined together in the Café Royal, not in the anaemic restaurant of today but in the full-blooded Café Royal of former days; its Victorian splendour was on the decline, but the crimson plush upholstering was still there, and so many long gilt mirrors hung on its walls that one could never get away from oneself. Well-known artists lent their patronage to the place and the waiters were foreign and therefore seemed more genuine. It had a carefree cosmopolitan air, and after three or four glasses of wine, a man could easily believe that he was dining in Paris.

We had finished a dinner chosen with considerable care by M. and he asked the waiter to bring us coffee and two glasses of brandy. 'I'll have coffee only if you don't mind,' I said.

'K.,why don't you drink?' he protested. 'Why on earth are you so abstemious?'

'I suppose it's because I always feel that alcohol is an attempt to get something for nothing. It's like spurring a tired horse instead of feeding it. It lifts you up for a moment or two into the heights and then dumps you down again at a lower level than you were before.'

'No, that's not the real reason. The true explanation of your distaste for alcohol is that you and I were brought up in a gloomy presbyterian atmosphere and, unlike me, you've never recovered from it. If you don't want brandy you must have something else. I refuse to drink alone.'

'Then I'll have a crème de menthe,' I said. 'I like the colour of it.'

The waiter exchanged a sympathetic glance with M. and then hurried off to execute his order. 'You make a great mistake, K.,' said M. as soon as he had gone. 'Either live like these people' (he waved his hand around and then glanced at a neighbouring table where two young men and two girls were making a great deal of noise) 'or else live in accordance with the principles of the work. Eat, drink and be merry, and get what you can out of life, or else turn your back on it and seek the Kingdom of God. All this morality tinged with emotion that people now mistake for religion is utterly useless.'

'I don't want to talk about religion,' I answered, 'but about what Ouspensky calls the work. Tell me where did he get all those strange ideas?'

'From Gurdjieff. He never claims them as his own but always acknowledges their source.'

'And from where did Gurdjieff get them?'

'I don't know and I don't believe that anybody else does,' answered M. 'He never spoke about the precise origin of the system, but obviously it comes from somewhere in the East. Gurdjieff's a strange man, K., quite different from anyone you have ever met. He's a wonderful actor and you can never be absolutely certain when he is romancing and when he is really telling you the truth. All that he has ever told us about the origin of the system is that he had many companions, that they made long journeys and suffered great hardships during their search for esoteric knowledge. I gather that they penetrated into little known parts of Persia, Baluchistan, Afghanistan as far as the frontiers of India, and even into the interior of Tibet. During these journeys they met wandering dervishes and all sorts of holy men, stayed in monasteries of various kinds, and were admitted into ancient brotherhoods. Afterwards they met together, pooled all the knowledge they had obtained in their travels and constructed out of it what we now call the system. You will notice that it makes use of certain terms taken from Western science. Gurdjieff has a very good working knowledge of science, and I always look upon the system as a sort of bridge that links up Eastern with Western learning. Because it establishes a connection between esoteric knowledge and modern science, it is quite unique and the most satisfying thing I've ever found. But why are you so suspicious about it all, K.?'

'What makes you say that?'

'I saw your expression suddenly change when I uttered the words "esoteric knowledge". We give ourselves away far more that we imagine we do. Why don't you like the word "esoteric"? What's wrong with it?'

'I suppose because so many frauds are perpetrated in its name.'

'Maybe. But hidden knowledge exists all the same. You forget that culture is much older than we imagine it to be and that long before men inscribed their knowledge in scrolls and papyri and books, they transmitted it from one generation to another by word of mouth. Take, for example, the ancient traditional knowledge found in the Upanishads and Vedas. I don't know what date Oriental scholars ascribe to these works but I believe that most of them believe that they were written sometime about the year 500 BC. Now if there is one thing of which we can be sure it is that this ancient wisdom of India was transmitted orally from teacher to disciple for many centuries before this date. Even if it had been possible to commit it to vellum or paper, it would not have been advisable to do so because teaching of this kind can only be really understood by those who had been specially prepared for it.'

'The idea of the initiate,' I murmured.

M. nodded. 'An initiate is a man who has reached a certain level of understanding and who is judged fit to receive more knowledge. In the ancient mysteries of Egypt and Greece there were the rituals and ceremonies performed in public, and, behind all this, a special teaching was given in private to those who were able to receive it. The ceremony did not confer on the initiate understanding. It was merely the outward and visible sign that he had reached a certain stage in his development. All through history we find the same sort of thing happening. In every country there appears at one time or another a teaching of a different character from its native philosophy and religion. I'll give you as instance of this the appearance of Orphism and Pythagorism in Greece and of the mysteries practised in the Island of Philae in Ancient Egypt. Both Orphism and the doctrines expounded by Pythagoras came from Egypt, and if we could trace them further back still we should probably find that they reached Egypt from somewhere much further East, or else from Atlantis. The ancient Hindu doctrine of the transmigration of the soul is to be found in all of them. All this means that there are two sorts of knowledge in the world, the ordinary knowledge to be found in books written by ordinary men and esoteric knowledge coming to us from some ancient and conscious source. Does that answer your question?'

'You mean that this knowledge has come to us from men on a higher level of being?'

'If it could be shown that it has not – it would be quite impossible to prove this – then we are both of us wasting our time. There are enough theories and subjective ideas as it is in the world and we have no need for any more.'

'Some of the ideas have a religious flavour,' I said, 'for example, the idea of the perfectability of man.'

'Of course they have,' he answered. 'Religion is founded on illumination, or knowledge revealed to the great religious geniuses in a state of higher consciousness. There can be different interpretations of truths, but not different truths, such as philosophical truths, religious truths, and so on. In their essence all truths are one. Have you read Jacob Boehme's imaginary dialogue between a disciple and his master in the *The Signature of All Things*?'

'No.'

'Then read it. It is written in the language of religion, but if it were translated into philosophical terms it could be read at Warwick Gardens. Boehme makes the disciple ask of his Master what prevents him from apprehending supersensual truth and the Master answers that it is his "thinking of self and his willing of self" and his imagination about himself that stands in his way. This is only another method of saying what the system says, that it is personality that prevents the development of a real and permanent self.'

'There's another thing I want to ask you,' I said. 'Why is it necessary to make such a mystery about everything? Supposing it be true that there are sources of knowledge other than science and literature and that every now and then this underground current of ideas comes to the surface, why must it be kept so secret? In other words, why shouldn't it be known that Ouspensky is holding meetings in Warwick Gardens? Why have I got to park my car in another street and sneak into the house as though I were a conspirator or burglar?'

M. laughed and lit another cigarette. 'It is not always easy,' he said, 'to disentangle the teacher from the Russian in Ouspensky. There is a good reason for not allowing indiscriminate talking about the ideas of the system, for talking is about the most mechanical thing in us and to forbid it is to bring it to our notice. We open our mouths and then, remembering that we are not allowed to talk, get a salutary jolt. Besides, we confuse not only ourselves but other people when we give an account of things before we really understand them. It's a good rule; but also there is no doubt that Ouspensky is unnecessarily scared about the police. In Czarist Russia, and still more in Bolshevist Russia, a meeting of intellectuals was likely to arouse suspicion, and I don't thing that he realizes that it is not quite the same here. Nor need we be surprised that he's over-careful when we remember all that he went through at the time of the Russian Revolution.'

'Is Gurdjieff the same?'

Again M. laughed but more heartily this time. 'Gurdjieff over-careful? Why I never met anyone who bothers so little about what people choose to think about him as he does. I don't believe he cares a damn for anyone. Anyhow, he knows how to handle the Paris police, and he's so clever that he can get anything he wants out of them.' M. looked at his watch and then called the waiter and asked for the bill. 'I'm sorry but I'll have to go,' he said, 'for I've got an appointment elsewhere.'

I was disappointed for it was barely half-past nine and I had other questions I wanted to ask. M. was the oldest of my friends but I knew better than to inquire why it was necessary for us to leave at such an early hour. 'Every man,' he had once said to me, 'should be allowed to have his own private life,' and I concluded that this engagement of his came under this heading. We parted at the door of the café.

CHAPTER V

IDENTIFICATION

WHEN talking about the ray of creation at the previous meeting Ouspensky made use of the concept of energy. He described the universe as made up of a network of vibrations passing in all directions, reinforcing each other, impinging on each other, opposing each other and imparting to each other the shocks required for the full development of the octave. The critical points at which these outside shocks were needed were called 'intervals' in the octaves, but there were also other points in this vast interplay of octaves that had to be studied, the places where vibrations became so concentrated that they formed 'worlds'. These 'worlds' were of very different magnitude, ranging in size from the great stellar galaxies, of which our Milky Way was one, to the planets, the earth and the moon. But it would be a grave mistake, he had said, to look upon these local condensations of energy, or 'worlds', as independent and self-contained entities. They should be regarded rather as focal points in an immense field of energies, or if we preferred this, as different parts of a single living organism. For its nutrition and growth each 'world' was particularly dependent on the next and greater world of which it formed a part and by which it was surrounded. For example, the earth received vibrations from the whole of the solar system and these vibrations were essential to its further development, just as the moon's future growth was particularly dependent on the energies it received from the earth. He ended by saying that in the economy of the universe nothing was lost and that energies which had discharged their function at one point in the universe were utilized elsewhere. The principle of the conservation of energy recognized by science was, he asserted, an equally important principle of the system. Everything in the universe fed on everything else and was in turn food for everything else.

In the next lecture I attended he no longer talked about vibrations or made use of the concept of energy but employed instead the concept of matter. 'This system,' he said, 'looks upon everything as being material, not only the phenomena that we see outside ourselves but also the psychical phenomena within us. It regards our thoughts, our emotions and our knowledge as being material, but material of a very different nature from that described by science. It subdivides matter into a great many different orders, ranging from the denser matters studied by science up to matters far too delicate and tenuous to be detected by the special senses. It is of these finer matters that psychological phenomena are made. This great range of matter, from the densest to the finest, is not only to be found in man but also in the great universe that lies around him. But there are other important differences between the system's and ordinary scientist's views of matter besides this. According to the teaching of the system, there is no such thing as inert and non-living matter. Everything in the universe is looked on as being alive, and this being so, no line of demarcation can be drawn between the inorganic and the organic. As well as being alive all matters have certain psychic and cosmic properties. The vital and psychic properties of the denser matters are of a very low order, but they nevertheless exist. For example, everything we know, even this table at which I sit, possesses some degree of intelligence. What does one mean by intelligence?' he asked.

As nobody offered any definition of intelligence, he answered this question himself. 'By intelligence we mean the capacity of anything to adjust itself to changes in its environment. If I place a heavy weight on this table, it will react to its increased load by a slight bending of its wood-fibres, and, having made this adjustment, it comes to rest. But if instead of placing a weight on the table I light a fire under it, it will not be able to get out of the way. It will not be intelligent enough this time to adjust itself to its environment. An animal can do better than this, for an animal in similar circumstances removes itself. A man has a still greater amount of intelligence, for he would know how to extinguish the fire and would not just let the table and room go up in flames. But the seeds of life, consciousness and thought are to be found everywhere, in every kind of matter, however low the order to which it belongs. Divisions into the living and the non-living and the mental and non-mental, the conscious and the unconscious are therefore only quantitative divisions and not qualitative ones.

There are fine matters,' he said, 'and dense matters; matters in which psychic properties are well developed and others in which they are only latent, and from the point of view of the system everything is material. Another way of expressing this is to say that all matters have vital, psychic and cosmic properties.'

There are times when a sword must be used to cut through the Gordian knots which entangle the web of philosophy, and it was obvious to me that Mr Ouspensky had gained a great advantage from his use of one now. With a single blow he had got rid of all those difficulties which result from the Cartesian division of the universe into matter and mind. The problem which had always puzzled me, and far cleverer men than me, the mind–body problem, had entirely disappeared. There was no longer any need to explain how two such entirely different entities as mind and body could meet and interact, for body and mind had become one. It was also possible now to connect two worlds which had hitherto insisted on standing aloof from each other, the world within us and the world without us. By replacing a dualistic philosophy by a monistic one, a great deal had been gained. It was true that the monism he had chosen was materialism, but it was materialism of an entirely new kind to the naive materialism advocated by certain scientists. Instead of degrading spirit to the level of matter, as they had done, it raised matter to the level of spirit. The whole universe had been invested with a new dignity, for it was regarded as being alive and shot through with intelligence and consciousness. Zeno's complaint that he could not understand how a dead and unintelligent universe could have given birth to a living, conscious and intelligent man was no longer relevant. The system taught that the universe and man were of the same nature and governed by the same great cosmic laws. Man was a microcosm in a macrocosm, a tiny replica of the great cosmos in which he lived.

Between meetings I thought a great deal about Mr Ouspensky's conception of the universe, sometimes finding much in it to commend it and at other times reacting against it and regarding it as visionary and rather absurd. In other words, there were 'I's in me that accepted Mr Ouspensky's ideas and others that remained staunchly scientific. But even when the pendulum within me swung in the direction of scepticism, I still continued to attend the meetings, and for two reasons. The first was that, however little I might get from the system's philosophy, I was undoubtedly gaining much from its psychology. My second reason for continuing my attendance was that I believed that it would be useful to me to be compelled to look at everything in an entirely new way. Just as there are habits of moving and of feeling, so are we wedded to customary modes of thought. These habitual methods of thinking eventually become so ossified and rigid that it is quite impossible for us to think of things in any other way. My education had been almost exclusively a scientific one, and science had disciplined all my thoughts. I felt therefore that it would do me no harm, and might even do me good, to be compelled to look at the universe from an entirely new standpoint.

But on further reflection I began to wonder whether the novel and astonishing ideas I had been given at Warwick Gardens were as new as I had first thought them to be. Fechner also regarded the universe as a great conglomeration of living souls with God as the supreme and all-embracing Soul. Unfortunately my ignorance of German closed his books to me, but I seemed to remember that he had said somewhere that when souls were viewed *inwardly* they were mental, but when seen from *without* they took the form of material bodies. He had also written that the smaller bodies were included within the larger bodies and that the Soul of God embraced them all. According to him life and consciousness were not evolved out of the lifeless and the unconscious, but the latter were degradations of the former. Many similarities could therefore be found between Fechner's philosophy, so far as I understood it, and the philosophy of the system. I also found many resemblances between the system and Whitehead's philosophy of organism. Whitehead regarded space as a vast arena for the interplay of cosmic forces and protested against the scientists' practice of making abstractions from it and then treating these abstractions as self-contained entities. He too denied the division of matter into the living and the non-living and insisted that the concept of matter must be fused with the concept of life. For him also the whole universe was alive and evolving, for ever 'plunging into the creative advance'. Yes, many of Ouspensky's ideas could be found in the works of other writers, even though they had not been so nicely dovetailed into each other, as in the system, so as to form a self-consistent whole. According to the system the universe was an immense hierarchy of living creatures existing on a great many different levels of being. There was to be found in it everything from organisms of so low an order that they seemed devoid of all life and intelligence up to that Omniscient and Divine Being who was the Creator and Preserver of everything that existed.

At one of his meetings Ouspensky drew on the blackboard a diagram which he called the Step-Diagram. Each step in this diagram represented an ascent from a lower to a higher level of being. On the lowest plane he placed the metals and minerals and then, as the diagram ascended, he placed on each step higher and higher forms of life, plants, invertebrates and vertebrates, culminating in man. Nor did the diagram end here for it continued to ascend, step by step, through higher and higher beings until it culminated in God, or the Absolute. This diagram reminded me of the hierarchies of beings that are described in the writings of both Liebnitz and Lotze. No, astounding though the cosmology of the system might be, most of the ideas contained in it could be found, in a less exact form, in other philosophical writings.

The universe portrayed by the system was a surprising and almost incredible one, but if one followed one's thoughts concerning anything far enough, they led to equally surprising conclusions. If it were not for the deadening effect that custom has on thinking, how astonishing it would seem to us to wake up in bed every morning and discover that we were alive, and not only alive, but conscious of being alive. No complete explanation of this familiar and daily event could be otherwise than astonishing and unbelievable. Science does not dispel mystery, or if it eliminates one mystery, it does so only by substituting for it a still greater mystery. Moreover, it is quite absurd to look upon scientific accounts of the universe as being restrained and sober accounts of it. Popular books about the recent discoveries in physics are as fantastic and as surprising as fairy tales. If it were not for the deadening influence of custom we would live, like Alice in Wonderland, in a perpetual state of surprise.

Two months passed before Ouspensky returned to what I had for so long been waiting for, his account of the evolution possible to man. He introduced this theme of the manner in which man might develop in the following way. 'Nothing in the Universe,' he began, 'ever stands still. It must either evolve, or else it must

63

degenerate, and this principle applies not only to man, but also to everything else, from the atom to the vast worlds of the stars. But evolution – and by evolution I mean the attainment of a higher level of being – never occurs anywhere mechanically; only decay and devolution can happen in this way. Tonight I want discuss with you the only form of evolution possible to a man, namely, conscious evolution. The best way of dealing with this subject is to describe first the seven different categories of man, starting with an ordinary man and ending with a fully developed man. The first three categories are to be found in ordinary man, that is to say, amongst men-machines. Man number one, number two and number three are all on the same level, and they are distinguished from each other by the centre which happens to be predominant in them. Man number one is a man in whom moving centre is very active, that is to say, a man who learns everything by imitation in the same way as a parrot or a monkey. In man number two emotional centre is well developed and his decisions are largely based on his likes and dislikes. Man number three is intellectual man, a man who always tries to base his decisions on logical thought. He is the man of theories and clever arguments, the bookworm and the scholar. All men are born either men one, two or three and they remain such as they are born. To man number four I shall return later. Men five, six and seven never occur naturally and are always the product of conscious work and of schools. The distinguishing feature of man number five is that he has attained inner unity. In him the innumerable fleeting "I"s which formerly made up his being have become, as it were, fused so as to form a single and permanent self. He has also attained real self-consciousness and he has occasional glimpses of higher states. Man number six has actually attained these higher levels of consciousness and his lower centres have made a connection with higher centres. This confers on him new knowledge and new powers, such as the power of controlled telepathy. Man number seven has attained full objective consciousness and will and he has developed as far as it is possible for human being to develop. Unlike men number five and number six he can never lose what he has gained, for it has become truly his own. He stands on the highest level of being on which it is possible for a man to stand, and he is a fully evolved and complete man. It must be borne in mind that each of these men possesses the knowledge that is appropriate to his level of being, for knowledge can also be divided into these seven categories. There is the ordinary knowledge of mechanical men one, two and three, and there is the knowledge of men number five, six and seven. What is true of knowledge is also true of art and religion. There is the religion and art of men number one, two and three and the religion and art of men five, six and seven.

'Man number four is a transitional form of man, that is to say, he is on the way to becoming man number five. He is distinguished from ordinary mechanical men one, two and three by the existence in him of a permanent centre of gravity. By this I mean that there is a fixed point to which he refers everything and by which he judges everything. He is a man in possession of a compass which enables him to determine the direction in which he is travelling. Mechanical men have neither chart nor compass, and, possessing nothing by which to steer, they drift first in one direction and then in another, the playthings of caprice and their desires. They do not possess one aim but many aims, as numerous as their different "I"s. Man number four's aim is to evolve, to become something other than he at present is, and this aim takes precedence over everything else. What helps him to reach his aim he calls good and what obstructs his efforts to reach it he looks upon as evil. He also possesses certain physical attributes which men one, two and three lack. He is still a machine, but he is a machine which knows itself to be a machine and which works far better than it formerly did. The centres of man number four are properly balanced, each doing its proper work without interfering with the work of other centres. But it must be remembered that there is nothing yet in man number four that is in any way permanent. He may easily lose everything that he has gained, because fusion, or crystallization, has not yet taken place in him.'

'Has he a self?' I asked.

'Not a permanent self,' he replied, 'but he realizes that there is something within him which may in time become a permanent self. A parable is used in ancient teaching which illustrates very clearly the various stages in a man's evolution. It is the parable of the house that is being prepared by the servants for the arrival of the absent master. This parable is to be found in the Gospels but

65

in an incomplete form. The house is in a state of chaos, and instead of the cook being in the kitchen, she is in the garden; the gardener works in the kitchen, the groom in the pantry and everybody is in the wrong place. Whenever a caller rings the front door bell a different servant opens the door, and in answer to inquiries declares that he is the master of the house. At last some of the more discerning of the servants realize how disastrous is the state of affairs and they agree to try to work together to remedy it. These more responsible servants or "I"s decide to elect a deputy-steward who will put everybody in his place and give orders. In time the deputy-steward is replaced by a real steward, and eventually, when the house has been brought into a satisfactory state, the master himself arrives. This parable illustrates the successive stages in the evolution of a man.'

'What stage have we reached?' asked a young man hopefully.

'One or two of the servants may have noticed that something is wrong with the running of the house,' answered Mr Ouspensky, 'but they have not yet realized it sufficiently to do anything about it. Work has not even begun with us.' The young man looked crestfallen, but Mr Ouspensky had more to say. 'Coming to lectures,' he continued, 'is not work and of itself it cannot lead to any change of being. All that I can give you here is knowledge. You remember what I said about knowledge and being? To impart knowledge is one thing but to bring about a change of being with the help of this knowledge is quite another thing. A change in the level of being can only be brought about by long effort and persistent struggle.'

'Struggle with what?'

'With mechanicalness and with sleep,' he answered; 'with all that keeps us where we are. Realize that this is not ordinary sleep from which we suffer. It resembles much more closely induced, or hypnotic, sleep. We have to find out next what keeps us asleep and, having discovered this, to try to get rid of these causes. The most important of them all is some sort of identification?'

'What do you mean by identification?'

'It is something that it is easier to see in oneself than to define. Identification means merging with something so completely that we completely disappear into it – for the time being we entirely cease to exist and become only a part of the thing with which we are identified. A man can and does identify with anything, with an idea, with an unpleasant emotion, with a person or a situation, with everything and with anything. At one moment be may *be* – he may be conscious of his existence – and then suddenly, his attention is attracted by something; he is sucked into it and from that moment he ceases to exist. He is no longer a person, but becomes the thing with which he is identified. The word we use in Russian for identification is the same word that we use to describe the merging of a small tributary with the main river. The rivulet disappears as a separate entity and becomes a part of something else. To struggle with identification is to make an effort to keep the feeling of "I" in the presence of some emotion, thought or situation which threatens to engulf us. Not-identifying has much in common with the non-attachment of the Buddhists. It is an effort to stand apart.'

'In other words, a sort of indifference,' suggested someone.

'That is precisely what it is not,' answered Ouspensky, emphatically. 'You could not have made a more misleading statement. What you call indifference is usually a negative emotion, and not to be identified is to be less asleep, more aware of oneself, the exact opposite of indifference.'

'But isn't every true artist identified with the picture he is painting and every actor with the part he is playing?' asked the lady who always assumed the role of protector of the arts whenever the subject of art was touched on. Because Ouspensky had said that a great deal of energy was lost by imagination, she was disposed to think that he was a Philistine, but by imagination he did not mean the creative imagination of the artist but uncontrolled imagination.

'Unfortunately an artist usually is,' answered Ouspensky, 'but if a painter were less identified with what he was doing, he would be more awake and, as a result of this, his painting would improve.'

'I always thought that the great geniuses were so absorbed in their work that for them everything else, including themselves, completely disappeared. Newton was so engrossed in his study of the laws of motion that he boiled his watch for lunch instead of an egg.' It was the schoolmaster who had spoken. Or was he a solicitor?

'Yes,' answered Ouspensky. 'He was completely identified and therefore more deeply asleep than usual.'

'But in spite of this identification he discovered the laws of mass and motion.'

'He might have discovered them earlier if he had been less identified,' replied the imperturbable Ouspensky. 'But we will leave the geniuses and their work,' he continued, 'and will consider something of much more importance, the identifications that keep *us* asleep. Probably the most troublesome of these are identifications with negative emotions and with people, with what they may or may not think of us. A man identifies so easily that he may become identified with so small a thing as an ashtray.' He picked the ashtray up from the table in front of him, looked at it and then replaced it. 'We spend our day passing from one identification to another.'

'You talked about struggling with identification,' said someone. 'How does one do this?'

'By trying to self-remember,' he answered. 'You remember the two-headed arrow diagram I drew on the board, with one head pointing to the object perceived and the other returning in the direction of the perceiver. See or feel the thing you are examining and at the same time be aware of yourself seeing or feeling it. So long as you manage to do this, so long as you maintain the sense of "I", you will not disappear; you will continue to *be* – to exist.'

'I find this very difficult,' said the lady with the long gold chains draped round her neck. 'I don't think that it will ever come naturally to me.'

'Of course it won't,' he replied. 'For it is against nature, against what has been happening in you all the years of your life. I never promised you that it would be easy. The only thing that is easy is to continue sleeping, and the most difficult thing is to awake.'

'If I were to cross Piccadilly Circus,' I asked, 'trying to self-remember, would I be more likely or less likely to be run over by a bus?'

'Less likely,' he answered without making any further comment.

'So far,' he continued, 'I've only asked you to try to do three things, to observe yourselves, to try not to express negative emotions and to try to self-remember. Now I add something else. Try not to become identified with things and more especially with

68

your favourite negative emotions. Everyone has his own favourite
negative emotion. Struggle to keep something outside it, even if it
be only the "I" that observes it. Don't be completely engulfed – try
not to disappear.'

'I think that I get most identified with people,' said a lady who
I had not noticed before. 'I've discovered, since I began to
observe myself, that I'm always wondering what they are thinking
of me.'

'A very good observation indeed,' answered Ouspensky. 'This
form of identification is so important that we have a special word
for describing it. It is called "considering". We consider people
too much, and by this I don't mean that we show a regard for
their feelings and welfare. It is the very reverse of this; we are
entirely preoccupied with what they are thinking of *us*, whether
they like us, whether they dislike us, whether they are giving us
our due or not and whether we are creating a good impression on
them. It is a form of inner servitude, a kind of inner bargaining,
the cringing of a lackey before his master. There is such a thing as
real regard for other people's needs. But we will not talk about
this at present. To know what is best for another person requires
much understanding, and to give him what he lacks and what will
help him is a form of "doing". It requires much understanding
and the exercise of will. But think about the various forms of identification which keep us asleep and make your own observations
when you come next time.'

At the following meeting Ouspensky did not continue his
discussion of identification but instead made two new divisions
of man. The first was a division into essence and personality.
'"Essence",' he said, 'is what a man is born with and what may be
called truly his own. "Personality" is what he subsequently
acquires as the result of experience and education. A small child
possesses only "essence", that is to say, certain physical character-
istics, tastes, desires, predispositions and potentialities. He is
what he is and does not pretend to be anything else. But he is
surrounded by a number of people whom he soon begins to imitate.
He receives also what is known as an education, and as the result
of these outside influences he soon acquires a "personality" which
grows far more rapidly than does his own "essence". So rapidly
indeed does this grow that it soon becomes the chief controller of

his life. "Essence" asserts itself only very occasionally as he gets older and in time it ceases to have any effect on his life, for by now "personality" has completely surrounded and obstructed any further growth of "essence". There are many grown-up people in whom "essence" has remained in the state at which it was when they were ten. This means they possess very little that is really their own and are almost entirely made up of the chance products of their environment and of their upbringing. "Personality" alone is active in them, and "essence" is reduced to complete passivity. These people are to be met with more frequently amongst the more highly educated sections of the community and amongst those living in towns. "Essence" is more likely to assert itself in simple people and especially in those who live on the land, and therefore closer to Nature. These people have fewer ideas, but what ideas they have are more real, and we usually realize this when we meet and talk with them. Although it is useful to divide man into "essence" and "personality", it is a theoretical idea rather than one of practical value. It is difficult and often impossible to distinguish in oneself what lies in "essence" and what lies in "personality". But in moments of danger and in our reactions to critical situations we sometimes reveal our essential qualities.

'The second division that I now give you is of greater practical importance to you and at the same time it is more difficult to describe. When a man has observed himself for a certain length of time and begins to realize the necessity for his making efforts to bring about some change, the character of self-study takes a slightly different form. So far he has been concerned only with the observation of details in himself, such as the working of his centres and the turning of certain small wheels in his machinery. Now he must begin to obtain a broader knowledge of himself as a whole. To do this he should learn to take, as it were, mental snapshots of himself at various moments of his life, snapshots which record simultaneously his postures, movements, tones of voice, thoughts, facial expressions and emotions. If he does this he will in time acquire a whole collection of these mental photographs, sufficient in number to enable him to discover that he is actually quite different from what he has hitherto believed himself to be. He finds that he resembles much more closely the person that other people have seen and that he is unlike the portrait that his own imagination has painted of himself. At those moments at which he sees himself clearly he will be aware of two persons in himself, the more real person who sees and the invented one who is now seen. The real person has the right to say "I", and to the imaginary person he can give his own name, whatever it happens to be. It is essential that this separation between the two men in ourselves, the "I" and the "Mr Ouspensky", the "I" and the "Mr X.", should be made, and it is from the moment that is is made that true work can begin. And if you succeed in doing this you will soon make a new discovery. You will find that it is the Mr X., in you that is always active. You will discover that you are completely in his power and that he does with you whatever he likes. If you are ever to move from where you are you must struggle with him, because he is your chief enemy and the great obstacle to your development.'

'Is essence the real "I" and personality the "Mr X."?' asked someone.

'If they exactly corresponded,' Mr Ouspensky relied, 'it would have been unnecessary for me to have made another division of man. Every idea in the system is connected with everything else, but I advise you to keep the ideas of Essence and Personality and of "I" and "Mr X." apart. But notice how you use the words "Mr X." instead of mentioning your own name. This almost always happens. A man tries to avoid using his own name when he is speaking about himself in the third person. When he makes use of this division I have just given you, he almost invariably says "the 'I' in me" and "the 'Mr Ouspensky' in me", "the 'I' in me" and "the 'Mr X.'", but never "the 'Mr Smith'", if his name is Smith. He seems to realize that Mr Smith is artificial, and of course nobody likes advertising the fact that his eye is a glass one or that his hair is a wig. He objects still more strongly to drawing attention to the fact that his personality is in great part a sham, which of course it is.'

The meeting ended with a further discussion of this new division which Mr Ouspensky had made and which he evidently regarded as of the greatest importance. He warned us not to fall into the common error of allocating to 'Mr Walker', 'Mr Smith' and 'Mr X.' everything that we disliked in ourselves and apportioning to the "I" everything that was praiseworthy. This

71

was a trick by means of which people in the work contrived to rid themselves of any feeling of personal responsibility for what they did. Whenever anything unpleasant in themselves was brought to their notice, they were able to exclaim lightheartedly, 'Oh, that is only the "Mr X." in me that behaves like that; it isn't really "I". But,' added Mr Ouspensky, just before he rose from his chair, 'there is scarcely anything in us that has the right to say "I", so it is cheating to speak in such a way.'

CHAPTER VI

IMPRESSIONS

IT would be tedious to follow the course of the meetings in Warwick Gardens and give the ideas of the system in the order in which we happened to receive them. It would not only be tedious but well-nigh impossible, for Mr Ouspensky often returned to subjects dealt with previously, but from a new angle. Sometimes he would interrupt a cosmological lecture in order to discuss how things on the scale of the universe affected man, and on another occasion he would answer a psychological question by referring us back to man's place in the universe. As our knowledge of the system increased, what we got from Ouspensky depended more and more on the questions we asked, and if these were not forthcoming he closed the meeting. He showed a strong distaste for certain types of questions, and when they were asked he brushed them aside with such comments as: 'Too many words'; 'There is and can be no answer to such a question'; 'I don't know what you mean'; or 'This is a good example of formatory thinking.' By 'formatory thinking' he meant that the question came from the lowest part of intellectual centre, that part of it which worked without attention and turned out words rather than ideas. I noticed also that poorly formulated questions were often accepted, whereas others more cleverly framed were left unanswered. At first I was puzzled by this, but I soon discovered that it was sincerity above everything else that he required of us. If a questioner showed a real desire to know something that seemed of practical importance to him, he obtained an answer, however badly his question had been put. But if the question had been manufactured without previous thought, and especially if the questioner repeated the words Mr Ouspensky had previously used, it was pushed on one side.

It is impossible to fix the precise moment at which new ideas cease to be just interesting and find a permanent place in our minds. Certainly no such moment can be named in this journey of mine through the puzzling inner world of thought, for the transition from one category to the other was so gradual that I never noticed it. Moreover, the value I placed on the system as a whole varied greatly at different times. Sometimes, and particularly after a meeting, I was fully convinced that through a fortunate accident I had come across something of inestimable worth, something that formed no part of the here-and-now in which I lived but that belonged to an entirely different locality and to another period of time. The whole thing seemed an anachronism. It was as though I had been strolling down Regent Street and had suddenly come face to face with an Old Testament prophet, or had sat down in a bus next to an alchemist who had pressed into my hand the philosopher's stone. To have come across this knowledge in this spiritually bankrupt century seemed to me to be miraculous. But twenty-four hours later I would turn a critical eye on the miracle and in dispassionate mood I would take careful stock of the whole situation. I was aware that I was inclined to be romantic and that when a man of this temperament is given a little suitable material he can do with it almost anything he likes. And how magnificent was the material with which I had been presented! Somewhere in the background behind the matter-of-fact Ouspensky lurked a mysterious Caucasian Greek, a Mr Gurdjieff, possessed of unusual psychic powers. Tales were told of his journeys over mountains and through deserts and of the terrible hardships he had endured in his lifelong search for hidden knowledge. There was everything in this material that the imagination could need, and I knew what it could do when it really got to work. But in the foreground was something I found it impossible to distrust – the critical mind of Ouspensky. By temperament he was a scientist and a philosopher and a man who made no claim to the possession of higher powers. He was somebody I could trust for had he not repeatedly said that nothing he told us was ever to be taken on faith? Everything must be submitted to test, and whenever such a test had been applied, I had invariably found that the knowledge he had given me was true. No, it was impossible to believe that my confidence in the system was misplaced.

The more I put into practice the psychological principles of the system, the more convinced I became of their value. I found, for example, that with their help I was able to overcome certain difficulties in my professional life, difficulties resulting from negative imagination. I no longer lay awake at night, as I formerly did, listening for the telephone to ring and for the night-sister to tell me that the patient on whom I had operated had suddenly collapsed. I ceased to wonder during the small hours of the morning whether it would not have been better for me to have done this rather than that, for by now I had fully realized the futility of such thoughts. And as the wastage of energy through worry and identification lessened I found myself able to do more and with steadily increasing efficiency.

At one of his meetings Mr Ouspensky emphasized this fact that we had only a certain sum of energy to expend every day and that it was essential to make the best possible use of it. This merely confirmed what I already knew, but Ouspensky now developed this important theme in a very interesting way. He likened man to a chemical factory which had been specially designed for the manufacturing of various kinds of energy. But man's trouble was that there was so much wastage in the running of this factory that very little energy was in the end produced. For the attaining of a high level of consciousness not only must all wastage be avoided but a far greater output of energy must be obtained by a more efficient working of the factory's machinery. But clearly it would be useless to produce more energy unless the leakage of it were first reduced, and this must be our first task. At present we used up energy on many worthless activities that would never give us any return. A few moments of negative emotion were quite sufficient to burn up energy that it had taken us many hours to produce, and afterwards we felt so depleted that it was impossible to make any further effort. It was imperative therefore to discover and to stop all these leakages.

He then turned from the problem of wastage to the problem of obtaining a higher output from the factory. Energy was produced, he said, from the food that we took into the body and there were three kinds of food. Science, he continued, recognized only one kind, namely, food introduced through the mouth. But the system regarded as food the air that we inhaled through the lungs and also the impressions we received through the special senses. It might be difficult at first to understand how the last-named could be looked upon as being food, but it should be remembered that whenever we received a message from outside, we at the same time received a certain amount of energy from it in the form of light rays, heat rays, or sound vibrations. Strange to say, the health of the mind and body was more dependent on the reception of impressions than of the other two kinds of food, for if a man ceased to receive them, he immediately lost consciousness. The impression we received from outside could be regarded as a driving belt which kept the wheels of our machinery in motion.

He then drew on the board a diagram which he called the three-storey factory. It represented the conversion of man's food into finer substances according to the principle of the law of seven. The lowermost storey was the abdomen, in which the digestion and refinement of the food taken in by the mouth occurred, the second storey the chest and the uppermost storey the head, the recipient of sensory impressions. With the help of data taken from a previous diagram known as the Table of Hydrogens, he showed the various steps in the conversion of the foods into finer substances. According to the law of seven, an impact or shock from another octave was required at a certain stage of this process if it were to continue. In the case of ordinary food, this shock was provided by the intake of air and the oxygenation of the venous blood in the lungs, but in the case of the other two foods, no shock was available. This meant that the conversion in still finer substances did not proceed as far as it otherwise might have done. He then made a statement of an extremely interesting nature. He said that so far he had been describing the finer chemistry of an ordinary man in a state of waking sleep, but that when a man was really self-conscious his inner chemistry was altered. If, at the moment of receiving impressions, he made an effort to 'self-remember', the impact made on him by these impressions was much stronger, and their conversion into finer substances proceeded a stage further. At this point somebody interrupted him and asked how an impression or perception could possibly produce anything in the form of a substance, and he was reminded that in the system everything, from a piece of coal to a thought or an emotion, was looked on as being material. Mr Ouspensky said that it was only because the philosophy of the system was a monistic one that he was able to draw on the blackboard a diagram showing the connection between psychological phenomena and the physical chemistry of the body.

After answering other questions, Mr Ouspensky returned to the study of man as a chemical factory built for the production of finer from coarser matters. These matters, he said, were required not only for the upkeep of the body but also for fuel. Each of the centres required its appropriate fuel if it were to work satisfactorily, but, as he had previously reminded us, the factory was run on very uneconomic lines. For man to evolve not only must all wastage be stopped but a much greater output of finer substances and fuels must be obtained. About the leakage of energy he had already spoken, and the diagram he was now about to put on the board would show us that self-remembering, or greater consciousness, was our chief means of increasing the output of finer substances. He then drew on the board a diagram which illustrated how the three-storeyed factory worked in the case of a man who was truly self-conscious, and who therefore produced a much greater output of finer matters.

Keeping to my plan of neither rejecting nor accepting ideas given at Warwick Gardens until I had had time to thing about them, I decided after the meeting to walk the whole way back to Harley Street and to recall everything I had just heard. The first idea I considered during this walk was that messages reaching us from the outside world acted as the driving belt to our machinery. This caused me no difficulty, for I remembered a case quoted by Michael Foster. In his *Physiology* he described a boy who was stone-deaf, blind in one eye and who suffered from a disease of the central nervous system which had almost completely destroyed his tactile sense. The boy's only links with the outside world were his one eye and a rather feeble sense of taste and smell. When his eye was closed he promptly went to sleep. I could accept Ouspensky's idea that man was dependent on the stimulations he received from the external world. But was it justifiable to regard sensory messages as food, or had Ouspensky been guilty of loose thinking in switching, as he had done, from the concept of sub-stances to the concept of energy? No, for the scientist frequently did this. In explaining the behaviour of light, we sometimes regarded light as vibrations and on other occasions we made use instead of Newton's corpuscular theory of light. In other words, we chose the concept which suited us best for painting different kinds of pictures of the outside world, just as an artist sometimes makes use of one medium and at another time of a different medium in order to obtain some different effect. No, Ouspensky had an excellent precedent for using on different occasions the terms substance and energy. It was difficult for me to regard thought as material, but then I had been brought up, as a Westerner, in a Cartesian climate of mind and matter. The Eastern philosopher probably found it quite easy to think of thought as matter for he started with an Eastern conception of matter. To him it came quite naturally to visualize various kinds of matter, from the coarse matters dealt with by science to the finest matters of the human mind. In any case it would be a very good exercise for me to escape for a time from my hereditary form of thinking, especially when the change brought with it the very considerable advantage of exchanging a dualist for a monist form of philosophy. The mind–body relationship problem would then no longer be a difficulty, and those two separate entities, the world within me and the world without me, would flow nicely together and become one.

But if it was true that impressions were food, there must be differences in the quality of this food, just as there was good meat and bad meat. This meant that good impressions were necessary to the health of the body, and, as I pondered over this idea, I began to see a connection between it and what is known as a 'change of air'. What did a doctor really mean when he recommended a change of air and sent his patient away from his home in Mile End to convalesce at Margate? Was it actually the change of air that made all the difference to the patient's health, or was it a change of impressions? If samples of Mile End air and Margate air were analysed chemically the results would be practically the same, except perhaps that there would be a small preponderance of dust in the former. Yet the benefit derived from the change was often very great. Might not this be due to the new health-giving impressions that the patient received while at Margate? His Mile End impressions had grown so stale to him that he hardly noticed anything in his surroundings. But translated suddenly to Margate, where everything was fresh, he drank in eagerly the sight of the sea, the cliffs, the gulls; he noticed everywhere new smells and received from his environment a hundred novel and invigorating impressions. Man cannot live by bread alone, but requires food for the whole of his being, for his mind and soul as well as for his body. I thought of the wretched nature of some of the foods on which the modern town-dweller subsists, foods that contained nothing fresh from the hand of Great Mother Nature: canned amusements from Hollywood; the Chamber of Horrors at Tussaud's; crime news in the press containing everything that was worst in human nature. Need we be surprised that a glimpse of something real works wonders in a man who has been sent to recuperate by the sea. And as I pondered over this idea of good and bad impressions, a disquieting thought came into my mind. I was a shareholder in Madame Tussaud's and, as such, made money out of the Chamber of Horrors! Next morning I telephoned to my brokers, instructing them to sell all my holdings.

During the following year the number of Mr Ouspensky's followers increased so much that he was compelled to hold more than one meeting a week. I was continually seeing new faces in the Thursday group, and although some of the old ones had disappeared, it had grown in size. Some of the new arrivals attended only one or two meetings, and this was not surprising when one considered the hard nature of Ouspensky's gospel. What most men wanted was immediate comfort and an easy path to perfection, two requirements which were not to be found in Warwick Gardens. It was obvious also that some of these new recruits arrived there with very definite views of their own, and, because their personal prejudices were not confirmed, they soon dropped out. A gaunt spiritualist had appeared a few meetings ago and had immediately asked Mr Ouspensky what his views of life 'on the other side' were. When Mr Ouspensky answered that it was of far greater importance to study conditions of life on this side, he was offended and withdrew. Another man had been distressed because Ouspensky insisted on using philosophical rather than religious terms, and, having inferred from this that the system was irreligious, he also disappeared.

Ouspensky made a reference at one of the meetings to the readiness with which new people left him. 'When anyone,' he said, 'hears that it is possible for a man to evolve he always concludes that he can start to do this from wherever he happens to be. He thinks that it is quite unnecessary for him to give up anything at all. If this were possible, it would mean that as such a man evolved everything in him would become bigger, his weaknesses as well as his strengths, both his faults and his virtues, everything that makes up that man. No, we must be prepared to destroy before we can begin to build, in other words, to get rid of much that stands in our way. When one goes to a tailor for new clothes one does not put on the new suit over one's old clothes. Yet some people insist on clinging to all their old ideas. Instead of making any adjustments themselves, they expect me to bring my teaching into line with what they think, with what they believe they already know. But why treat truth as though it were something exceedingly delicate and fragile? We must be brave enough to put everything we have into the crucible and when it is withdrawn from the furnace, we shall find that the gold we have put in is still there. Nothing that is true will have been lost.'

In expressing his ideas Mr Ouspensky often made use of metaphors drawn from the old alchemists, and on one occasion he likened a man to a retort filled with a number of different metallic powders. If the retort was tapped or lightly shaken, the distribution of the various powders in the mixture was changed and one that had previously been below might now appear at the top and vice versa. If any permanence or unity was to be imparted to such an accidental mixture as this, it must be fused by applying fire to the retort. An amalgam would then be formed, an amalgam that not only had a permanent constitution, but that possessed new properties as well; it would be perhaps a good conductor of electricity, or be capable of being magnetized. The fire by which a man could become indivisible and attain a permanent "I" was friction, or the struggle between "Yes" and "No" within him. So long as he gave way immediately to all his desires no fusion could possibly take place and unity would never be obtained. But if for the sake of some great and enduring aim, he struggled with these desires, fusion might occur. We must turn to our advantage the various difficulties supplied by life, utilizing them for the achievement of our aim. By doing this our losses and difficulties might be turned into profit. 'Sometimes,' Mr Ouspensky said, 'it is necessary to increase difficulties intentionally, or even to manufacture them.'

'How?' asked someone.

'This is done in esoteric schools. The teacher sets a pupil some task to perform, a task which necessarily entails the pupil having to struggle with his own personality, that is to say, to work on himself. The task forces him to go against what is called his "chief feature", or chief weakness. The teacher knows what this chief feature is and he therefore sets his task accordingly. If the pupil tries to avoid this work or fails to carry it out, it means that he has no real desire to struggle with himself and is therefore useless. In schools, difficulties are often specially created for the pupils, and their reactions to this artificially produced frictions are carefully watched.'

How strangely do our memories treat us. Ouspensky's reply brought back to my mind words that had been spoken to me many years ago, words that up till now I had forgotten. I suddenly recalled how, before I came to any meetings, I had spoken to M. about his life in the château at Fontainebleau, and how he had shown a marked disinclination to answer my questions. All that he had said was that work at the château was based on two principles, those of producing in the pupils exhaustion and irritation. That the 'Forest Philosophers' should be exhausted was easily explained by the late hours they kept and by the hard work they were compelled to do. But up till now I had never been able to understand what M. had meant by the principle of producing irritation in them.

I was just on the point of asking a question on this subject when I suddenly changed my mind. It had become apparent to many of us that Mr Ouspensky no longer visited Mr Gurdjieff in Paris. Something had happened which had induced him to break off his long connection with Gurdjieff, his teacher, but what this source of disagreement was nobody knew. There were rumours, but what, after all, are rumours but products of the imagination. Nor was Ouspensky's reason for leaving Gurdjieff any concern of ours. Even if we owed our knowledge of the system originally to Gurdjieff, it was not he but Ouspensky who was our teacher. So, much as I should have like to inquire of Ouspensky about the method of work employed at the Prieuré, I decided not to do so but to bring the subject up with M. the next time I met him.

CHAPTER VII

FALSE PERSONALITIES

THE year 1933 saw the beginning of a new phase in Ouspensky's work in London. For some months he had been stressing at his meetings the impossibility of a man's achieving any tangible results by working alone. Not only was it difficult for him to arrive at self-knowledge, but he was unable to make those super-efforts which were necessary for any change in the level of his being. This being so, some sort of school was essential, and by this he meant an organization under the control of a properly qualified teacher. Ouspensky said that such schools had always existed in the past, but that nowadays they were becoming more and more difficult to find. He recalled to us that in 1914 he had gone to India in search of a school and that although he had not found what he was looking for, his journey had not been entirely fruitless. He obtained clear evidence of the existence in India of schools, but not of the kind he personally wanted to join. They either demanded of the newcomer too much faith or else they were schools of a religious nature. The World War then made it necessary for him to return to Russia, and there, purely by accident, he met Mr Gurdjieff, the man from whom he had obtained all the knowledge that he was now passing on to us. It was obvious that Gurdjieff had acquired this system of knowledge in some school, or more likely in several schools, but he would never disclose its precise origin. All that he would say was that he was not alone in his search but with several others and that they had travelled extensively in Egypt, Persia, Baluchistan, Afghanistan, the Chitral border of India, Tibet and China. He said also that they had suffered incredible hardships and that some of his companions had died in the course of their wanderings. The origin of the system must therefore remain unknown to us unless Gurdjieff revealed it, which was very unlikely. Ouspensky then went on to say that up till the end of the last century schools could be found in Europe, generally disguised as something else. There was every reason to believe that the builders and sculptors of Notre Dame belonged to an esoteric school. To the world they appeared to be only masons, architects and labourers, but behind this façade of their outer work, they carried on their own inner work. In the past some disguise was necessary in order to protect the school from the persecution of a jealous Church. There also existed during the last century a so-called school of painting in Europe of a similar nature. This worked at Düsseldorf during the summer and in winter moved south to Italy. There was evidence of Ibsen having been at one time a member of it, but it was probable that he left it because the duties and attractions of life proved too strong for him. In *The Master Builder* he seemed to be giving his reason for not being able to continue the inner work on which he had embarked. His mouthpiece was the Master Builder himself, who, when reproached for the abandonment of his former high ideals, replies that he has renounced the building of churches in order to make homes for ordinary men and women.

There was much discussion on this subject of schools in meetings and it eventually became evident to us that Ouspensky intended to form some sort of organization to assist his work. He made it clear to us that this organization could not claim to be a school, but that it would be a means of studying school methods. It would also supply what was now necessary to us, more intensive work, working in groups, more rigid discipline and obedience to rules. The first step would be to acquire a large house somewhere in the neighbourhood of London, with enough ground to provide opportunities for outdoor work. The search for this had begun.

What was considered to be a suitable property was found a few months later in the form of a large house with about ten acres of land situated at Hayes. Madame Ouspensky, who had previously been at Gurdjieff's château, the Prieuré, had arrived in England some months previously and she now took up residence in the new house, where she was joined by some of the more senior of those who attended Ouspensky's lectures. These formed a nucleus around which the new organization was gradually formed. During the weekends more and more of us went down to Hayes to work either in the house or the garden.

There could be no doubt that working together in groups was a great help to self-study, for a man has much greater difficulty in detecting his own weaknesses than in seeing the weaknesses of others. By working in a group he often makes the unpleasant discovery that the very faults which he sees and dislikes in his fellow-workers exist also in himself. Ouspensky explained to us that group work is made more effective when the groups have been so arranged by the teacher as to be made up of people of different types. This inevitably produces friction between its members and the personalities of the different individuals forming the group are thereby rendered more conspicuous. In this way each member of the group may act as a mirror in which some fellow-worker may see himself. Moreover, by working together and pooling the results of self-observation, a far greater amount of material can be accumulated for common use than when an individual works alone.

Mr X. and I certainly rendered our personalities conspicuous to each other when we set out one fine Sunday morning to perform the simple work of beating rugs. But beating rugs only seemed a simple job to one of us, myself. For me it entailed nothing more complicated than laying the rug on the lawn, picking up opposite corners and beating the rug as hard as possible with a walking-stick or a cane. It was an entirely different proceeding for Mr X., who had carefully thought out what appeared to me to be an unnecessarily elaborate plan. Instead of simply spreading out the rug on the lawn, it was to be suspended from a cord passing between two neighbouring trees. Having carefully explained the plan of campaign to me, Mr X., who invariably did most of the work in any communal task, went back to the workshop to select a suitable rope. He was a very long time away and eventually reappeared with a clothes-line that was certainly long enough, but of a rather dubious thickness. Having debated the subject of its tensile strength at great length, and having mutually decided that risks must be taken even in such a homely enterprise as the beating of rugs, we stretched our cord between the two neighbouring trees, only to find that it was tied far too low. When the heavy rug was thrown over it, the cord gallantly held, but it was so weighted down that it scarcely succeeded in raising the rug above the level of the ground. It would tedious to recount the various efforts we made to remedy this defect; the search for steps, the suspension of the cord at a greater height, the difficulties we encountered in getting the rug over it, our success in overcoming this particular and the final breaking of the rope! Mr X. and I learnt a great deal that morning not only about different types of rugs but also about different types of men.

Few people realize how clearly they reveal themselves in everything they do, and the reason for this blindness is very clear. When our attention is drawn to our manner of thinking, feeling or moving, we are surprised that it should excite comment. For us it is not merely *our* method of thinking, or of doing, but also the right way of thinking or doing. We are indeed at pains to explain to the critic the reasonableness and correctness of the pattern of behaviour to which we are bound. What is true of the beating of rugs may be equally true of the philosophy at which we have arrived; this may be equally subjective. Nor was this the only kind of lesson that could be learned from working in the grounds or house at Hayes. Whatever we did had to be done with the strictest attention, and the customary method of working was often deliberately changed. For example, a person who was accustomed to work at a certain pace altered his natural rhythm and worked either faster or slower. His effort to work differently, and the difficulty he encountered in maintaining the change, made him aware of his mechanicalness, just as a swimmer drifting down a river will discover the force of the current by turning in the opposite direction and swimming upstream. 'Everything *happens* in us' was Ouspensky's favourite theme and now that we were trying to *do* things differently we discovered the truth of this saying. Few things are more difficult for a man to realize than the fact that he possesses no will and it is obvious why this should be so. 'But I did what I wanted to do,' he exclaims when his mechanicalness is pointed out to him. 'How can you say that I have no will?' Yes, he has done what his various desires (and not an independent will) have compelled him to do and over these desires he exercises little or no control. So it is only when, for the sake of a single persistent aim, he turns against the current of his mechanical desires that he discovers what is the real meaning of the word 'will'.

But when I look back on those days of psychological discovery it is not work with my colleagues in the garden, the house, or the fields that is recalled, but the figure of Madame Ouspensky, around whom everything and everybody revolved. I catch glimpses of her coming unexpectedly into the garden, standing there for a few moments watching us at work, and then disappearing again into the house. From the distance I hear her voice in the kitchen and note the accentuation of the noises coming from there with the increase of activity which her presence generally provokes. I see her at the head of the long dining-room table around which we gathered for our meals, or later in the day, when outdoor work is over, I see her seated in the drawing-room. She is listening to somebody who is reading to us aloud from a book which recounts the journeys of Gautama the Buddha, or else she is talking to us about our failure to struggle with our mechanicalness. Madame has what is usually known as a presence, the bearing of a *grande dame*, and I could readily picture her receiving her guests at one of those great house-parties for which Czarist Russia was famed, or else presiding over some glittering *salon*. Not that she would have enjoyed such a setting, but she would have managed to adjust herself to it. Nothing would have flustered her and she would have known exactly how to act in any unforeseen social emergency. But she would have been popular only with few of her guests, for she had an uncanny capacity for seeing what lay beneath the surface and, having seen this, she did not hesitate to name it. But a gift that might well have caused trouble in the old social life of Russia was now being used for our gain, and although most of us feared her, we realized how valuable was her help. For why had we all gathered here in this strange establishment at Hayes instead of enjoying a week-end game of golf or working at home in our own gardens? We were here because we wanted to discover the personalities to which we were slaves and if anybody could help us to do this and to escape from our thraldom, it was surely Madame Ouspensky. She was an expert in the stripping off of masks, in the detection of hypocrisy and fraud, and in separating the real from the counterfeit.

Madame Ouspensky had only a very imperfect knowledge of English and I had great difficulty in understanding her, but fortunately her gestures were extremely eloquent, and from them alone I often caught the gist of what she was saying. There were members of the group who had a good command of both Russian and English and to these she would sometimes apply for help when we failed to grasp her meaning. Turning to one of them she would say: 'He not understand. You explain.' Then after an awful pause there would be hurled into the quiet of the hushed room the comment that had previously been mercifully blanketed: 'Madame says that you only repeat Mr Ouspensky's words and that a clever parrot can be trained to do that,' or 'Madame says that you are a warning to us all and quite useless.'

I regretted that I had difficulty in interpreting her speech, for whenever I did manage to catch her words, they were so brightly coloured and so apt that they left a deep imprint on my mind. I can still recall many of her phrases. The chattering of one person to another would be described by her as 'the pouring of emptiness into the void' and a theoretical discussion of the system as 'singing about the work', or as 'talking about high questions'. She was always suspicious of fine words and required of us tangible signs of a determination to work. If, after a certain period of probation, these were not forthcoming, then she would be utterly ruthless. 'Why you come here?' she would ask. 'You come here because you think this a country club, but Madame has not time for idle people who show no desire to work. You not come again.' And if any person had been so dismissed, it was only with the greatest difficulty that he could gain permission to reappear.

I can remember her description of the false personalities which we were attempting to protect from her assaults. She likened the false personality to a huge hot air pie which the owner carried about with him on a tray in order to exhibit it to his friend and have it admired. But possessing only a very thin crust his pie had to be guarded very carefully for otherwise the pretentious thing crumbled at the slightest touch and revealed to the world its emptiness. Why, she asked, should we take so much trouble and care about a thing so utterly worthless as a personality? People were not so easily taken in by appearances as we thought, and, in any case, they were so preoccupied with their own personalities that they had not time to take notice of others. 'Madame,' she would say, 'is not interested in what is artificial in people. She is only interested in what is real in them, in that small part of them which sees what they actually are and has a desire to become something else.'

Sometimes I would look with dispassionate eyes at the scene in the drawing-room at Hayes and would take stock of the whole situation. What an amazing scene it was and how dumbfounded my friends would be if they were suddenly to be transported here! What would they be able to make of it all? How puzzled they would be to explain that we, reasonably intelligent people, were sitting here at the close of a hard day's work at the feet of woman who seemingly did nothing but insult us. She had just referred to one of us as 'a piece of meat' and to another as a person 'completely devoid of mind'. She had also reminded us again that this was not a country club and we had no right to treat her house as such. A country club! Had there ever been a club in the whole of the world's history run on such lines as these? What would the friends who my imagination had smuggled into this room make of this strange and bewildering scene? They would make nothing of it but would be speechless with surprise. What was happening here ran counter to everything else in life. It was 'the work' and entailed a struggle against the whole current of mechanical existence. It was an heroic attempt on the part of a few people to oppose the mighty forces of nature. 'Was this venture on which I had embarked utterly quixotic?' I sometimes asked myself. 'Were we tilting at windmills or were we engaged in an enterprise which could bring positive results, small no doubt, but nevertheless worth obtaining?' Before answering my own question I would look round the room and my survey was generally reassuring. The people assembled here were more genuine than those I met elsewhere; they spoke less often for effect and more from themselves. But whether this venture ended successfully or in failure, whether it was reasonable or irrational, I realized that I no longer had any choice. I must go on with it.

During the summer months our meals were often taken out of doors. In a part of the garden conveniently near to the kitchen the ground formed a natural amphitheatre looking out on to a meadow, and Madame gave instructions that four tiers of seats should be built along its sloping flanks. There, whenever the weather was fine enough, we sat in rows, balancing our plates on our knees like children at the annual summer outing. On the flat ground in front of us were placed four or five small tables, the one on the extreme left for Madame, that opposite it on the right for Mr Ouspensky, should he elect to join us instead of eating as usual in his study, and those in the centre for visitors from London.

It was no trivial ordeal this, that those newcomers were to undergo when they seated themselves in front of us all and in full view of Madame. If they knew anything at all – as they usually did – about the purposes of the establishment at Hayes, they were aware of the fact that in their every action, in the way they sat, in their facial expressions, in the manner in which they ate their food, their personalities were about to be revealed. It would be useless for them to compose their features from outside and to attempt to assume the external demeanour of a person who was in a good state, for Madame would not be taken in. I had often tried this myself as I walked up the drive to the house and it had always ended in miserable failure. For Madame always penetrated the pose and revealed the man or woman that lay within. Not that the rest of us, sitting on our hard benches, were rendered immune from her attention by the presence of visitors, for from time to time she would turn in our direction and would say such things as: 'Mr W., do you see yourself now in Major T.?' Miss O., do not forget,' and with a few gestures she would mimic a peacock displaying its tail, or a cinema star posing for her photograph. And so clever was her mimicry that everybody, including often her victim, would laugh, but the latter not very comfortably.

But it may well be asked, 'Why was it necessary to be so preoccupied with something that every man and woman must inevitably possess – a personality?' Why had it to be seen, and what was the point of trying to get rid of an attribute that is native to all mankind? It is natural that such questions should be asked, especially now that a Personalist Movement has started, the aim of which would seem to be to cultivate what the people at Hayes were apparently trying to destroy. The explanation of the contradictory aims of the Personalists and of the group at Hayes is to be found in the different meanings attached by them to the word 'personality'. The Personalists believe that in spite of the multiplicity of its parts, the personality is a unity with a character and a value of its own. In their opinion, therefore, it is something worthy of being developed. The followers of Ouspensky had an entirely different conception of man and attached a different meaning to the word 'personality'. This meaning was much closer to the root word from which the word 'personality' was originally derived, namely, the 'persona', or mask, behind which the old Greek actors played. The personality, in the sense in which it is used in the system, is not the real inner core of man but something that he wears. But unfortunately there is an essential difference between the masks of the Greek theatre and man's personality. Whereas the Greek actor used his 'persona' for his own purposes, it is our personalities that use us. We have to play the roles which our personalities dictate to us. Our aim was therefore not so much to destroy as to bring into subjection the part of our being that had seized control of us and to render it far less active. The personality is a bad master, but it may be made into a useful servant. But a servant to whom? it may be asked: to the 'I', or Self, that must eventually be created if the confusion that reigned within the house of our being is ever to give place to harmony and order.

There was another reason why personality had to be first seen and then rendered less arrogant and less active. It is through the distorting glasses of our personalities that we always see everything not as it is but as it appears to us to be. Nothing is viewed clearly or objectively, but always through and intervening haze of likes and dislikes, partialities and prejudices, obsessions and idiosyncrasies. How can we ever hope to see things and persons as they are unless we can manage to get rid of this quotient of personal error? How indeed can we obtain any more knowledge, and more especially that kind of knowledge that comes through intuition, or direct perception, rather than through the intellect, unless the personality can first be got out of the way. The so-called intuition of a man controlled by his personality is only a manifestation of his prejudices and bias, and nothing more than this.

So for the sake of a distant aim we accepted the unpleasantness of having our personalities revealed. Mr Ouspensky had always warned us that the truth about oneself was often painful and so it generally turned out to be, whether that truth were self-found or uncovered for us by somebody else. The fact is that we live mostly in our imaginations and, like industrious silkworms, spin round ourselves gorgeous chrysalises of silk. It is therefore bound to be unpleasant when rude hands tear all this spun finery of ours to pieces and reveal to the world that there is nothing inside it but a very ordinary grub. Yet there are compensations attached even to this. Having been seen, and having seen oneself as one is, there is no longer need for recourse to that troublesome art of 'saving face'. Men who have lost all their money can no longer be robbed.

The evenings that brought to a close the many hours of work done in the garden or meadows of the small estate at Hayes are amongst the happiest of my memories. Whenever it was warm enough we had supper out of doors, and some of the cooking for this was done over fires, or in brick ovens built in the open. I can still see Captain H., late of the Grenadier Guards, crouching on the ground and holding a rapier-like weapon over the flames. He is preparing *shashlick* for the evening meal and has a number of fragments of salted beef threaded on to his immense skewer. The great majority of the day workers have returned to London and the few that remain for supper are now like the members of a great family waiting for their parents to join them at the evening meal. Muscles and minds are luxuriously relaxed and we await with eagerness the signal that supper is about to begin. At last a gong sounds somewhere in the house and Miss C. struggles out of it overburdened with a large tureen of soup. She is followed by Madame Ouspensky and Mrs M. and by others who have been preparing dishes in the kitchen, and when we have all taken our seats the father of the family, Mr Ouspensky, often appears. The serious work of the day is over, but Madame is never completely off-duty, and few people entirely forget that she is there. At any moment they may catch her eye looking in their direction and they may suddenly become the object of her attention. But if she speaks to them, it will probably be in a lighter vein than earlier in the day and what she says will be followed by a spreading ripple of mirth. Nobody is in a position to feel superior for there is no saying who may not become the next target for her wit.

It was at such moments as these that Madame's gift of mimicry was appreciated most. She would recall a number of different things that she had noticed, out of the corner of her eye, during the course of the day; Mr N. arriving late for lunch and hoping not to be seen; Miss D. dusting a room in the manner of a lady dabbing her face with a powder-puff; Mr M. grinding coffee beans in the kitchen and expending on this task as much energy as would be required to raise a heavy bucket out of a deep well. And having announced her programme, she would enact each scene with the skill of Ruth Draper. M. had once said to me that those who deal with serious things must never lose the capacity to laugh, and I now realized more fully the truth of these words. We were serious about things that other people might have thought trivial; we often laughed when they would have been serious. Our values were in process of being changed and whilst some things had become much more serious for us, we no longer bothered about many of the things which formerly we regarded as of the greatest importance. We were beginning to acquire the ability to laugh even at some of the of the more ridiculous sides of ourselves.

CHAPTER VIII

THE HOUSE AT VIRGINIA WATER

By 1936 the property at Hayes had become too small for our needs, and Mr Ouspensky decided to look for a much larger house and a great deal more land. Farming could then be undertaken, even if it were only on a very small scale. He agreed that it would be difficult to find anything suitable sufficiently near London to allow of easy access, but said that it would be advisable to investigate everything that came into the market. Eventually a large house, which had become too big for its owner to run, and a hundred acres of land were purchased in the neighbourhood of Virginia Water. Many repairs had to be done before the new property could be used. These were begun immediately, and with very little outside help the whole property was gradually brought into a satisfactory state. By now we had different kinds of specialists working with us, among them architects, engineers, electricians and carpenters. Under their skilled direction a great many expert jobs were accomplished. Three months later Mr and Madame Ouspensky moved in, accompanied by a much larger number of permanent residents than had ever been housed at Hayes.

During the week-ends as many as a hundred people sat down to meals, and everything else was now carried out on a correspondingly large scale. Mr and Madame Ouspensky aimed to make us, so far as this was possible, into a self-contained, self-supporting community. This they succeeded in doing and at the end of two years we were growing our own wheat, milling our own flour and baking our own bread. The kitchen-gardens and orchards provided us with all the vegetables and fruit we required, and in order that none of the latter was wasted, a fruit drying apparatus was built in a shed. This department was placed under the able charge of a professor of Oriental languages, perhaps because Buddhists are vegetarians. To each of the permanent residents was assigned some special responsibility, and when the rest of us arrived from London, we worked under their expert supervision.

But in Madame's words, 'every plus has its minus'. Much as we had gained from moving into larger premises, many of us were conscious of having also sustained a loss. One obvious loss was that we saw less and less of Mr and Madame Ouspensky, and as a consequence obtained from them less help. The feeling of belonging to a family had disappeared and been replaced by the feeling of belonging to an institution. Yes, there could be no doubt that some of the things which the older among us greatly valued had been lost by this very rapid increase in the size of our community. Otherwise work at Virginia Water was very similar to work at Hayes, except that new activities were being added to our list, such as the felling of timber, the erection of a Heath Robinson type of sawmill, sheep and dairy farming, ploughing, sowing, reaping and market-gardening.

I had long ago noted that Madame's approach to the system was different from that of her husband. Mr Ouspensky was by nature a philosopher and a scientist, and although he recognized the similarity between many of the system ideas and those taught by all the great religious teachers, he deprecated the use of religious terms when discussing the system. If one employed them he would point out that there were four different paths to man's evolution; the ways of the fakir, of the yogi and of the monk, and in addition to these three 'classical' methods, a fourth method, the method which we ourselves were studying. Each way had its own technique and its own terminology, and to mingle the terminology of one with the terminology of the other would only have resulted in confusion. He therefore never allowed his hearers to equate the Absolute with God, or to substitute the word 'spirit' for the higher parts of the mind. 'These are religious terms,' he would say, 'and as we are not studying religion, we shall not make use of them.' With Madame it was otherwise. She had very little knowledge of science, but she had a strong feeling for religion. Not only did she make free use of religious words in her talks with us, but she arranged for us readings from a number of religious books; from the *Sayings of the Buddha*, from the *Bhagavad Gita*, from the *Apocrypha*, from the books of the Old Testament Prophets and from the writings of the Early Christian Fathers. She also had various extracts made from the Tao and from Sufi literature, and after these had been read she would draw our attention to the similarity of the truths they expressed with the truths of the system. There was, for example, no better description of the various stages of identification than that to be found in the *Philokalia*, a description which was so apt that it was clear that the old Desert Fathers had carefully studied identification in themselves. So also did she unearth a great deal that was relevant to the study of the system in that work of Sufi genius, the *Mathnawí* of Jalal'uddin Rumi. From this book we had many readings, and no better description of Madame's relationship to us could be given than that found in this particular work. The following extract has been taken from the 'Story of the Housewife Basting Peas'.

> Look at a chickpea in the pot, how it leaps up when it is subjected to the fire.
> At the time of its being boiled, the chickpea comes up continually to the top of the pot and raises a hundred cries.
> Saying, "Why are you setting the fire on me? Since you bought (and approved) me, how are you turning me upside down?"
> The housewife goes on hitting it with the ladle: "No!" says she: "boil nicely and don't jump away from one who makes the fire.
> I do not boil you because you are hateful to me: nay, 'tis that you may get taste and savour,
> So that you may become nutriment and mingle with the (vital) spirit: this affliction of yours is not on account of (your) being despised."
>
> (*Mathnawí*, Book III, verses 4159-64)

I personally gained much profit from these readings taken from the sacred literatures of the world. Not only did they help me to see the great psychological truths incorporated in religious teachings, but they imparted to the ideas of the system a certain warmth which previously they had lacked. They also drew religion, philosophy and psychology closer together in my mind, with advantage, I believe, to my understanding of all three.

Had she wished to do so, Madame could have extracted a whole sermon out of Jalala'uddin Rumi's story of a housewife basting peas. Situated as man is in a universe in which everything is affected by everything else, it is impossible for him to insulate himself from his surroundings and enjoy what he calls 'free will', for he must inevitably be controlled by what is stronger than himself. But he has been given a small measure of choice. He can select the influence under which he prefers to live and can place himself under the power of something higher or of something lower. His position is very similar to that of an Indian being swept down a swift river in a frail birch-bark canoe, who by means of skilful and hard work with his paddle can manoeuvre his tiny craft into a current which will carry him in the direction in which he wishes to go. But if a man has the desire to form part of something higher he must first be suitably prepared for this change.

> "I do not boil you because you are hateful to me: nay, 'tis that you
>   may get taste and savour,
> So that you may become nutriment and mingle with the (vital)
>   spirit ..."

There were, of course, certain points at which the teaching of the system and the doctrines of Christianity seemed to come into conflict. One of the commonest criticisms of Ouspensky's teaching made by newcomers of a religious type was that it encouraged a man to think too much about himself. Instead of considering the welfare of others, Ouspensky required him to be concerned only with himself; with his personal aim, with what helped him to attain that aim, with what stood in his way, with his own thoughts, movements and feelings, in short, with everything that pertained to himself. Surely, it was said, this was the antithesis of everything which Christ taught. Christ had told his disciples to take no thought for themselves but to think only of others. So little indeed had they to be concerned with their own safety and comfort that, on being buffeted on the one cheek, they were to turn to their assailant the other. They were to love not only their friends but also their enemies.

Ouspensky listened to such criticisms as this with a patient smile and at the end of it quietly asked the speaker whether he was capable of following Christ's precepts. Could he turn his other cheek to the man who had just struck him? Could he manage to love his enemy? The answer was in the negative, and then Ouspensky explained that if it had been 'yes', this would have meant that the speaker claimed to be on the same level as Christ's disciples, a very high level indeed. He reminded him that these precepts had not been given to the multitude but to his disciples for they alone were capable of following them. True Christianity meant far more than the acceptance of certain doctrines; it entailed 'doing'. To be a real Christian one must be able to live in accordance with the principles laid down by Christ, and this being so, there were very few people who had any real right to call themselves Christians.

He then answered the criticism that the system encouraged a man to become even more egocentric than he was by nature. 'It does the very reverse of this,' he said. 'It encourages him to struggle with his own petty and personal desires, with everything that stands in the way of further development. Before he can be in any position to help others, he must first help himself. How can a man whose own garden is in a state of wild disorder give advice to his neighbour? Yet this is what everyone does, for it is far pleasanter to look over the fence at one's neighbour's garden and tell him what is wrong with his flowerbeds than to attend to the weeding of one's own. This teaching is the reverse of what you imagine it to be. One of the principles it lays down is that it is the duty of all those who have obtained any benefit from its teaching to pass on that teaching to others. What he has received he must return.'

He gave a similar answer to a question on the subject of the efficacy of prayer. The real problem, he said, was not whether prayer was or was not efficacious, but whether one was able to pray. 'There are many different kinds of prayer,' he continued, 'but the commonest kind is some sort of petition. When such petition prayers are examined, more often than not they take the form of a request that two and two shall not make four. Certain actions of the petitioner have been followed by certain inevitable results and he prays that this sequence of cause and effect shall be broken. This is a kind of prayer that can give absolutely no results for causality reigns in the world within us as well as in the world without. What a man sows that also shall he reap. The truth is that one must learn to pray just as one must learn to do everything else. If we learn to pray then we may get certain results which will be the direct consequence of our ability to pray.'

There is another point at which the system seems to come into conflict with Christian doctrines. It looks upon man as a machine reacting automatically to its physical and psychological environment and composed, as all other machines are, entirely of matter. The philosophy of the system has the appearance therefore of being a strictly materialistic and deterministic one. But on closer examination this similarity between the teaching of the system and scientific materialism disappears. In the first place the system's conception of matter is very different from that of the scientist. According to the system all matters have psychological as well as physical properties, the finer matters possessing these properties in a very high degree. The system also teaches that the denser matters are often permeated by finer matters, as a sponge may be permeated with water in which oxygen dissolved. Its teaching therefore has certain affinities with the now discredited scientific theory of vitalism, the 'vitalistic principle' being represented in the system by finer matters. Nor is the system's teaching strictly deterministic. It allows of the possibility of a man becoming other than a machine. By the use of certain methods something may be produced in him that is capable of withstanding the impact of outside happenings, and even of withstanding such a catastrophic event as the decay of the physical body. This concession of the system that death does not necessarily entail the total extinction of a man makes it possible to reconcile its teaching with that of Christianity. Christians have always been compelled to subscribe to a dualistic philosophy because they have believed that an immaterial spirit alone is capable of surviving death; but the philosophy of the system is a monist one in which the spirit is represented by finer matters. It may well be that the finer substances which permeate the being of the more highly evolved man are not destroyed by death.

An examination of the system suggests that it has come from different sources and it is obvious that one of these sources was of a religious nature. It contains the idea of different orders of body, a teaching that the theosophists have recently revived, and a teaching that was formerly a part of Christian doctrine. I recalled all that Mr Ouspensky had said on the subject of man's finer bodies. At one meeting he drew on the blackboard a diagram to illustrate their development. The first body of man was the ordinary physical body, or in Christian terminology, the carnal body. The second was the astral body, or what was called in the Christian literature the Natural body; the third the Mental or

Spiritual body; and the fourth the Causal or Divine body. But, as Mr Ouspensky pointed out, there is a vital difference between the teaching of the system about these higher bodies and that of theosophy. Whereas theosophists credited all men with the possession of these four bodies, the system teaches that the last three of them only exist in a fully developed man.

This comparison of the ideas of the system with those of the great world religions helped me, I believe, to reach a better understanding of both. The terms used by the system and by the religions differed but the statements they made were generally the same. There appeared to be a particularly close relationship between the ideas of the system and the doctrines of the mystery religions, such as Orphism and Pythagoreanism. While thinking about this similarity I was reminded of what M. had said many years ago when he likened esoteric knowledge to a subterranean current of ideas which occasionally broke through to the surface and then, after a certain time, took an underground course again. Nobody knew where Gurdjieff had obtained this system of knowledge, but there could be no doubt that it was very old and that it had been transmitted to us orally through a long line of teachers and disciples.

A few years after we had settled down at Virginia Water an entirely new activity began there. In his earlier lectures Mr Ouspensky had discussed the different methods of development possible to man. He had talked to us about the way of the fakir, who, by means of terrible physical sufferings, eventually gained will over the physical body; he had described the yogi as travelling by the intellectual way, that is to say, by the control of the thinking mind. He had contrasted these two methods with the religious or emotional way. The monk worked primarily on the emotional centre, by means of prayer, meditation and strict obedience to his religious superior, the abbot. All of these three paths to evolution demanded of the disciple obedience to authority and retirement from life, but in the fourth way, the way which Gurdjieff taught, retirement from life was unnecessary. Life provided the pupil with the material he needed, and, unlike the fakir, the yogi and the monk, the traveller by the fourth way worked on all three centres simultaneously. He sought to gain control over his thoughts, his emotions and his movements. This description of the fourth way gave rise to a number of questions. It was obvious to everybody that self-remembering entailed control over thoughts and that the struggle with mechanical desires meant work on emotional centre. But in what way, it was asked, were we working on moving centre? To this question Mr Ouspensky had replied that at present very little attention had been paid to moving centre but that later on a means of working on it would be arranged. It was now that he kept his promise.

We were reminded that Gurdjieff had brought back from his travels more than a system of knowledge. He had returned also with music, a number of complicated physical exercises of a special kind and certain ancient Temple dances. Mr Gurdjieff was indeed generally accepted as the greatest authority on sacred dances in Europe, and it was in his capacity of author of a ballet, 'The Struggle of the Magicians' that Ouspensky had first met him. The exercises that we were now about to study had been specially designed to assist the gaining of control over the moving centre.

I have always prided myself on my attention and much of my professional reading and writing has been done at odd moments in buses, tubes and trains. But Mr Gurdjieff's exercises showed me very clearly that my capacity to direct my attention wherever I liked was less than I had believed it to be. The exercises in which I now began to take part were such that they could not be performed mechanically but only by maintaining the strictest awareness of what one was doing. Heady, body, arms and legs often moved in different rhythms, and when it seemed natural to turn in a certain direction the exercise often dictated that one should turn in the opposite direction. To make things still more difficult a number of intellectual exercises were added to the movement exercises, such as counting backwards or repeating lists of disconnected words in a foreign tongue. The slightest wandering of the attention threw the whole affair out of gear, and the fact that something had gone radically wrong became as obvious to the pupil as it did to the teacher. The exercises acted therefore as a very sensitive indicator of the performer's inner state and recorded the flickering of his attention, much as a revolving cylinder of smoked paper, used in a physiological laboratory, records the beat of an animal's heart.

It was difficult at the end of a hard day's work in London to drive some twenty-odd miles into the country in order to take part

in these supremely difficult exercises. At such times the flimsiest
excuse seemed to provide a valid reason for not going. A whole
conversation would start up inside me; the fog was getting thicker
and in the neighbourhood of the river it would be worse still; I
ought to drop in at the nursing home after dinner and make sure
that everything was all right; next day would be a heavy day and
it would be a mistake for me to start it depleted of all energy. On
those evenings I found a dozen reasons for remaining in London
but the strange thing was that however fatigued I might be when I
began Gurdjieff's difficult exercises I always drove back to London,
so full of energy that I had no desire to go to bed. 'Why,' I would
ask myself, 'should I huddle down under the bedclothes now that
I am feeling at my very best and am capable of doing almost anything?' I can offer no satisfactory explanation of the energizing
effect of these exercises but can only record what invariably happened. Six months later a great evening party was held at the
house at Virginia Water and everybody was invited to it in order
that they might see these movements. An immense marquee was
erected on the lawn and a stage was erected. On this, the special
movements and dances were performed by a troupe of about thirty
of the most expert men and women, dressed in Eastern costumes.

There is a right size not only for individuals but also for aggre-
gations of individuals, and if the group does not conform to this
size, it may become unserviceable for the work for which it was
originally formed. Mr Ouspensky now began to complain that the
number of his followers was unsatisfactory for his purposes and
that he had two alternatives. He could either cut down the size of
the group and carry on more intensive work with a smaller following, or else he could open the door wider and allow more people
to enter. In the latter case the character of the work would inevitably change and a new form for it must be devised. Eventually he
decided on a second course, a decision which meant that we must
find a larger meeting-place than the house in Warwick Gardens.
But this was not the only change that his decision entailed. If we
were to admit a great many new people, attention would be
drawn to our activities, and it would be necessary, he said, to form
a society and give it a suitable name. Unknown activities and
nameless societies always aroused suspicion, and it would be
advisable to form some properly constituted association and then

find some label for it. Ouspensky said that this was particularly necessary in such troubled times as those through which we were passing, when all undertakings of a secret nature would be likely to be carefully scrutinized by the police.

There was much discussion about the sort of society that could be formed and about the name it could be given, but eventually it was decided that as psychology enjoyed a great prestige at that moment, the word 'psychological' should be incorporated in its title. Eventually our difficulties were settled and a society was formed to study all those psychological systems of the East which taught the doctrine of metempsychosis, or the perfectability of man. It was given the awkward title of Historico-Psychological Society.

Everything was done in as orderly and business-like a manner as possible. A large house in Hammersmith containing two big studios and a hall capable of seating three hundred people was first purchased, and the articles of the society were then drawn up by one of our solicitors. Nominally the new association was to be under the direction of a Council, Ouspensky's name appearing in the prospectus only under the heading of official lecturer. Actually he supervised everything that had to be done, from the alterations to the premises to the purchase of the smallest of its new electrical fittings. The Executive Council was merely a façade behind which he worked. There existed a rather vague idea that lectures on appropriate subjects would be given to the public later on in the large lecture hall, and that those members of the audience who seemed suitable would be told afterwards about the real nature of our work. It was also believed that other activities, such as the formation of a library, the starting of various lines of research and the publication of a journal, might eventually be undertaken.

None of these grand plans were fated to be fulfiled. Man is surrounded by forces of which he has no knowledge, and events on a vast scale were slowly moving towards their predestined end. The state of man's world was steadily deteriorating and it was clear that humanity was soon to be subjected to the ordeal of war. We had long known that this was bound to happen, not on account of the appearance of a psychopathic demagogue amongst the Germanic people, but because man in his present condition is unable to escape from the great forces which bring about wars.

Those preparations which it was possible for us to make had long been made, and all that we could do now was to await the breaking of the storm.

CHAPTER IX

THE END OF OUSPENSKY'S WORK

On the morning of 3 September 1939, I stood on the high ground in front of the Virginia Water house watching the children clambering up the path leading from the lake. It had come, and the time of waiting, the growing tensions, the feeling of physical heaviness in the air were at an end. We were at war. I was conscious of a certain sense of relief, but whether this was due to the morning sunshine and the beauty of the scene, or whether it was comparable to the relief felt when a thunderstorm which has long been hanging overhead has actually broken, I could not tell. I had just been listening to the thin unmusical voice of Mr Chamberlain delivering its message to the British nation at war, and now from the distance came the wail of sirens. The first raid of World War II was apparently about to begin, and the children were hurrying to the basement of the house for shelter.

Fifteen years had passed since the conversation with M. that had started me off on a journey I was still pursuing. I could remember M.'s very words: 'There are great disasters ahead of us, K. There will be wars, political unrest, revolutions, and all on such a vast scale that everything that humanity has managed to build up may well fall in ruins.' And I, believing in the automatic progress of man, had refused to accept these words and had talked glibly about the League of Nations and the outlawing of war. How naive I had been to imagine that men who had no control over themselves and their passions could, by appending their signatures to a scrap of paper, outlaw war. 'It won't work,' he had said, gripping my arm so as to impart greater weight to his words. 'It cannot possibly work, and in a few years the League will not exist.' Was it prophecy? No, it was calculation; the tracing of effects from causes. Why should tomorrow be different from today or from yesterday in the absence of any alteration in the machinery of life? How can wars be banished from the earth by a flourish of pens while inwardly men remain the same? Well, I knew better now than to suppose that by means of any external ritual men can escape from World War II, III or IV. 'And they had brick for stone, and slime they had for mortar. And they said, Go to, let us build a city and a tower whose top may reach unto heaven; and let us make us a name, lest we be scattered abroad on the face of the whole earth' (Genesis 11:3–4).

The tower had fallen and these children were hurrying to the well-timbered room that had been prepared for them in the basement. I would go and see whether they knew how to adjust those newfangled gas-masks, for a doctor was supposed to know all about them. I felt more like offering the children my apologies than my advice. What a commentary it was on the mismanagement of the world by their elders that they should now have to be shown how to adjust their pig-like snouts.

The plans that had been long prepared were now put into action. Madame had made arrangements for as many of the London women and children as possible to be accommodated in the house and in the various cottages of the estate. There would be no difficulty about feeding them, for a big underground store had been dug near to the house, and this concrete food stronghold was now choc-a-bloc with hams, dried fruit, jars of salted butter, sugar, oatmeal, flour and provisions of every kind. When people have long known, beyond any possibility of error, that a war will come, it is easy for them to show foresight. Our preparations had been completed, and all that we could do was to mitigate, so far as was possible, the sufferings caused by war.

But however well prepared we were for this inevitable event, it soon became obvious that our activities, as a group, would have to be seriously curtailed. Occasional meetings were held in London, and those who had not been called up for national service still continued to work on the farm at Virginia Water. Later, with the intensification of air-raids, difficulties became so great that all London meetings had to be cancelled and work at Virginia Water severely curtailed. Finally Madame Ouspensky decided that it would be better for her to leave England. She had only one motive for living, and if work could no longer be continued here, she must go wherever it was possible. She had sailed for the United States with all those who were able to accompany her, and, a month or two later, she was followed by her husband. With the departure of the two teachers group work came to an end.

How scared I had been of that word 'group' fifteen years ago, and particularly scared of a group which was reputed to be building an ark in Kensington. But now I had a better understanding of the symbolic meaning of the word 'ark'. It signified a refuge in a time of catastrophe, and at this very moment 'a flood of waters was upon the earth'. What had we achieved by all our building? We had gained the advantage of knowing the direction in which we wanted to travel, and that was a bigger asset than most people believed. We knew that what had happened could not possibly have been averted and that it was useless to be filled with regrets for the past or with anxieties about the present; we had confidence that when 'the waters were abated' Ouspensky would return to England and organized work would be resumed. Finally, we possessed a map by which to try to steer through the uncharted flood that covered the earth. These were far from being negligible gains.

The war years slowly passed, and from time to time news reached us from across the Atlantic. We heard that an estate had been bought in New Jersey and that the Ouspenskys had been joined, not only by those who had been able to leave England, but also by many Americans. Meetings were being held in New York and an entirely new chapter in Ouspensky's work had begun. Then there came news of a less favourable kind, to the effect that both he and Madame had been ill. Another year passed, the war came to an abrupt end, and at last there arrived the news for which we had long been waiting. A letter announced that, although Ouspensky was far from well, he had sufficiently recovered from his illness to make it possible for him to travel to England in a few months' time. The letter added that the establishment in Hammersmith should be prepared for his home-coming. This surely meant that activity would soon be resumed and that there was no longer any danger of everything coming to an end. Hitherto, we in England had had to face the possibility that the movement which had been started in Moscow as long ago as 1917, that had spread thence to Paris and from Paris to London, would gradually become feebler and feebler and finally cease. This would mean that nothing would remain of the system of knowledge which Gurdjieff had found at such cost to himself and his companions, nothing beyond a few fading memories in the minds of some six or seven hundred people scattered over the face of the earth. Because we ourselves had gained so much from this teaching, we felt that it must be saved from this fate. We were, of course, aware that Gurdjieff himself was still alive, but as he must now be very advanced in years, we had little hope of his being able to safeguard the future of his own teaching. It was of the utmost importance that Ouspensky should return as soon as possible to England, and we were greatly relieved by the news that he would soon be here.

Ouspensky returned, but not the Ouspensky of old. There stepped on to English soil a man whom we hardly recognized, a man who had aged by twenty years since we had last seen him, a man on whom Death had already set his mark. We afterwards learnt that up till the last moment it had been doubtful to everybody in America whether he would be able to undertake the journey, but he regarded England as his home and was determined to return. He was driven from Southampton to the house at Virginia Water, where he retired to his old room. He spoke very little, but it was obvious that his mind was deeply engaged on some problem.

Two months later he met his followers at a meeting in the big hall of the house at Hammersmith, and we could see from his replies to our questions that he had evolved some entirely new plan for the continuation of the work in London. But it was equally obvious to us that he would never have sufficient strength to carry this plan through, and the idea of calling other meetings to hear more of what he proposed to do was abandoned. He retired to his room at Virginia Water, seeing only a few people and speaking very little to anybody. When he did talk it was generally on the subject of memory. He advised people to go back into their pasts and to try to recall everything that had happened to them, and more particularly to recall those cross-roads at which it might have been possible to have taken a different turning. He called this 'reconstructing' one's life, and it became clear to us that his mind was occupied with the idea that had always been of the greatest importance to him, Eternal Recurrence.

The idea that life describes a circle in the fourth dimension, the point of death coinciding with the point of birth, is a very old one. It existed long before Nietszche popularized it, and a reference to it can be found in Justin Martyr's *Dialogue with Trypho, the Jew*. In this book a discussion is recorded in which Justin Martyr remarks of certain philosophers: 'They affirm that the same things shall happen always; and further, that you and I shall again live in like manner, having become neither better nor worse.' This remark is introduced quite casually into the discussion without any preface or subsequent explanation of it and this undoubtedly indicates that it was no new idea even in those far-off days. Ouspensky himself has dealt with eternal recurrence in *A New Model of the Universe*, and he has also made it the theme of his only novel, *Strange Life of Ivan Osokin*. It was an idea that could be approached intellectually from a consideration of the nature of time, or else emotionally from what one felt about one's own life.

Like all answers to the insoluble riddle of birth and death, eternal recurrence cannot be discussed or argued about in the ordinary simple way in which people usually treat such subjects. The riddle of life and death is closely associated with the riddle of time, and the common view of time is that it is a long line along which we travel until we reach the end the end of it. This leaves no place in it for recurrence, but drives to the only possible conclusion, namely, that what has been can never return. Ouspensky had his own views on time which he has expounded in *A New Model of the Universe*. He had also had moments at which he was filled with the feeling that 'all this has happened before'. One of these moments had occurred when, as a very small boy, he was taken by his mother to his first school. They found themselves in a long corridor and his mother did not know in which direction to turn in order to find the headmaster's study. But Ouspensky knew. He told his mother that further along the corridor there was a passage down which they must go. At the bottom of it there were two steps and a window through which would be seen the headmaster's garden, with lilies growing in it. There they would find the door they were looking for. It was as he had described it.

During the last few weeks of his life, the idea of recurrence was continually in his mind, taking precedence of everything else. Not only did he appear to be recollecting the past, but he insisted on being driven to all the places that had been the scene of events in his life since he had first arrived in England. Ill though he was, he was driven to Hayes and Sevenoaks and to various villages in Kent and Sussex in which he had formerly stayed. He gave the impression of being a man who had set himself a definite task, for the accomplishment of which there was but little time. This work had to be completed, however much it might cost him, and complete it he did. What was his reason for inflicting on himself so much suffering and fatigue? Was it only in order to be able to revive certain memories which had faded, or did he want to look again at old scenes in the hope of stamping them so firmly on his mind that he would be able to recognize them again in another cycle of recurrence? He had often said that if a man could recollect, and had also will, he would be able to alter the whole course of his life. Was this in his mind while he was visiting these scenes of former events? Nobody will ever know, for he spoke very little to those who were with him. Having accomplished all there was to do, and realizing that further struggle was useless, he returned to his room and died.

A memorial service was held at the Russian Church in Palace Road, which all who could do so attended. When personality finds itself in unfamiliar surroundings for which it possesses no suitable role, it becomes less active and may even lapse into silence. Then some deeper part of us may begin to speak and to take charge of us. As I knelt awkwardly on the floor of the church, holding a lighted candle in my hand and listening to the Russian choir, I thought of the man who had been my guide for so many years. From him I had learnt all that I now valued so greatly, and, realizing how much I owed him, I was filled with a deep feeling of gratitude. When we doctors take our Hippocratic oath, we swear to hold our teachers in the medical art equal to our parents, and Ouspensky had taught me a far more difficult art than medicine, the art of living. I would therefore reverence his memory as my Hippocratic oath required me to do and think of him in the same way as I thought of my parents. And it was particularly fitting that he should be linked in my mind with my parents, for as I had always respected, but never really known, my father, so had I always respected, but never really known, Ouspensky. The relationship which had begun in Gwendyr Road over twenty years ago had been maintained up to the end, the relationship of teacher and pupil. As human being and human being we two had never met. To what was this absence of any real warmth in our friendship due? I knew that I had been inclined to consider with him, but I could not attribute everything to this, for I had the feeling that few of his followers had ever succeeded in coming very near to him. It was true that, after several glasses of wine at one of those all-night sittings at Hayes or at Virginia Water, he had sometimes become more intimate with us, but next day the old relationship was always resumed. His interest lay in ideas, in the study of higher dimensions and cosmoses, in the theory of eternal recurrence, in philosophy and science rather than in people. We were of interest to him chiefly because we illustrated principles in the work or were representatives of types. No, Ouspensky and I had never met on any footing other than that of master and pupil. Deep gratitude and respect were the tributes that I paid to him at the memorial service in the Russian Church.

Did Ouspensky's death mean that the work had come to an end in this country, or could we find some means of carrying it on? This was the all-important question that had now to be faced. The prospects for carrying on Ouspensky's work in England were not very favourable, for at no time had he made any provision for its continuation after his death. He had never delegated the smallest responsibility to any of his followers but had kept the direction of everything in his own hands. There was nobody in England capable of taking his place, nobody even with enough authority to summon a general meeting. Nothing remained of the organization Ouspensky had built up except two large houses and the executive council of a society which only existed on paper, the Historico-Psychological Society. By mutual agreement this council now met, discussed the situation at great length and decided that a letter should be sent to the only person who had any authority to act, Madame Ouspensky. The letter was sent, and because the reply received two weeks later was ambiguous, three of the council left for America.

While waiting for their return we had plenty of time for taking stock of the situation. Ouspensky had given us knowledge of great value, for the preservation of which we were all responsible. We felt ourselves to be under the obligation of passing it on to other people, in the exact form in which we had received it, without anything having been abstracted from it or anything added to it. What made the system so valuable was that it was a synthesis of philosophical, religious and scientific ideas. This was what we

Westerners badly needed, for here analysis had run riot; philosophy had lost all connection with religion, and religion with science. Everything was in the charge of specialists working in an ever increasing number of separate departments. In contrast to this, the system formed an integrated whole, and the study of one part of it assisted the understanding of another part of it; its cosmology threw light on its psychology, and vice versa; its religion and its philosophy were one. With its help much that was formerly obscure could be understood. The Gospels, for example, had acquired a new life and meaning for me. They look upon man precisely as the system looked upon man, that is to say, as an unfinished product capable of reaching a higher level of being by the use of certain methods. What was required of him was that he should cultivate in himself the higher at the expense of the lower, die on one plane in order that he might be reborn on another. Thus and thus only could he attain the Kingdom of Heaven which lay within him.

What a mess the theologians had made of that profound psychological treatise, the New Testament, and what a still worse mess the Freudians had made of everything that pertained to religion. This was chiefly because they failed to understand that there were different levels of knowledge, just as there were different levels of understanding, consciousness and being. It was from this that all those absurd controversies between science and religion had arisen, from this and from the failure of people to understand that the intellect and the emotions spoke with different tongues. Whilst the intellect used the language of words, the emotions spoke the language of symbols and legends and myths. Truths of immense value to mankind were to be found in the old Bible stories of the Garden of Eden, the building of the Ark and of the Tower of Babel, truths which could only be found if these stories were understood psychologically and not literally. Untold damage had been done by the interpretation of the language of one centre in terms of the language of another, and this mistake was still being made. It was its insistence on this difference of language, and the emphasis it placed on different levels and on different scales, that made the system so helpful to one. It stated that what was true of phenomena on one scale, or level, was not necessarily true of phenomena on another scale or level, thereby anticipating the modern principle of relativity. Yes, the system was a map to be used whenever one had lost one's bearings and did not know in which direction to turn, a map on which everything of real importance was marked.

The message for which we had been waiting was of such a potent nature that it split the council of the Historico-Psychological Society in twain. It was a very simple message: 'Get in touch with Mr Gurdjieff in Paris'. There were some who believed that to do this would be an act of disloyalty to their old teacher, who, for reasons unknown to us, had parted from Mr Gurdjieff many years ago. There were others who saw the position in a different light. The work, they said, was something which existed on its own merits quite independently of those who taught it. Why Ouspensky had parted from Gurdjieff was, they said, not their affair, but that the work should continue undoubtedly was. Those of us who interpreted the situation thus had no hesitation in acting on Madame Ouspensky's advice.

CHAPTER X

GURDJIEFF

On the evening of 2 October 1948, my wife and I found ourselves gliding down a long winding corridor of darkness towards the reeling lights of Le Bourget. Then the aeroplane flattened out, the landing ground beneath us regained horizontal position and with the gentlest of cushioned bumps we touched ground and sped along the broad tarmac pavement towards the brightly lit hangars. We were in France and at the gateway of a great adventure, a meeting with Gurdjieff. Gurdjieff; how often we had wondered what he was really like, this unknown man whose name was so familiar to us. And tomorrow we would be calling on him! It was as difficult to realize this, that we had come to Paris for the express purpose of visiting this legendary figure, as it would be difficult for a reader of the *Thousand and One Nights* to realize that he was about to drink coffee with Haroun-al-Raschid. We had arrived too late for anything to happen that night, so we had an excellent dinner – how tasty the food at that little restaurant was after ten years of rations – and retired early to bed. I was tired after the journey and soon found myself slipping down warm slopes of comfort towards a haven of sleep, with the word 'tomorrow' sounding feebler and feebler in the depths of my mind.

As E. V. Lucas has said: 'The pleasures of entering and re-entering Paris in the evening is only equalled by the pleasure of stepping forth into the street next morning in the sparkling Parisian air and smelling again the pungent Parisian scent and gathering in the foreign look of the place.' No air could have been more crystalline and sparkling than the air we breathed next morning as we walked to the meeting place we had arranged with A., a café in the Avenue Wagram only a few hundred yards from the Arc de Triomphe. A. had come back from America direct to France, and it was the telegram he had dispatched three days ago that had summoned us to Paris. Within forty-eight hours of receiving it, we had managed to renew our obsolete passports, to make arrangements for money with the bank and to secure seats on a plane. But there was more than the invigorating air and autumn sunshine of Paris to excite us as we walked slowly towards the café, for that very morning we were to meet the man to whom we owed all the ideas of the system, the strange and enigmatical Mr Georgi Gurdjieff. What would he be like and how would he receive us? Were the stories that were told about him true or had he been grossly maligned? Was he really as old as Rom Landau had tried to make out in that article of his in *God Is my Adventure*? A dozen questions were forming in my mind, but no doubts as to the fitness of our decision to come to Paris. Whatever others might think, for me it was as right as it was inevitable that I should be here.

I had come in search of knowledge of a kind that is not to be found in books, and now that Ouspensky was dead, it had to be obtained direct from Gurdjieff. What sort of man he was, why Ouspensky had left him, whether the rumours I had heard about him were true or not true did not matter. I was no longer content to rely on the opinions of others but must see for myself. One can sup with the devil himself if one uses a sufficiently long spoon and I had no doubt of my ability to discriminate between a good man and an evil one. I must see Gurdjieff.

A. was already at the café when we reached it, and the three of us sat down together at a vacant table and ordered coffee. He had a great many interesting things to tell us as we sat there watching the Parisian crowd passing along the pavement in front of us, so much news indeed that our supply of coffee and aperitifs had frequently to be renewed. He began by saying that Mr Gurdjieff had received R. and him very amiably on their arrival from America, and that since then they had seen a great deal of him. 'You have the feeling,' he added, 'that he takes you on to the palm of his hand, weighs you and then either accepts you or else puts you back in your place. We cannot of course be certain, but we have a general impression that we have managed to pass this preliminary test of his, and that everything is going to be all right. He also seems to be genuinely interested in what is happening in London and to be encouraging people to visit him here in Paris. Captain B. has already arrived with a lot of his people, the A.s are expected tomorrow and T. has been with us for over a week. But I must provide you with a rough sketch of the general background, and then you will be in a better position to understand the relationship that seems to be establishing itself between ourselves and G.'

A. then gave an account of what had happened to Gurdjieff during the last twenty years. He said that in 1924 Gurdjieff had visited America to organize a branch of his institute there and also to give demonstrations of his movements and dances. He had taken with him a troupe of well-trained pupils, and, in spite of the absence of the usual preliminary publicity, the demonstrations had met with considerable success. He had returned then to Fontainebleau with the intention of revisiting America in the following year, accompanied by a still larger troupe. But a terrible motor accident had occurred soon after his return to France, an accident from which any ordinary man would have died. It took him over a year to recover from his injuries, and as he lay in bed struggling back towards health, he arrived at the decision that in the future his work must take an entirely new form. He decided that the transmission of his ideas by personal teaching must now be curtailed, and that he must embody everything in a series of books. He had no experience of writing and had never wanted to be an author, but it was now essential that he should become one. Having arrived at this decision he set about his new task of authorship with characteristic intensity and vigour. He wrote in his flat, in the cafés of Paris, by the roadside during his motor tours, anywhere he happened to be and at all hours of the day and the night. Previously his followers had enjoyed access to him whenever they saw him sitting in a café, but now he was always occupied and they had to await his invitation to sit down at his table. After ten years of unremitting work he produced not one but three series of books, and some of the chapters of the first series were now being read at his flat. This first book was a strange allegorical work called *Beelzebub's Tales to His Grandson*, with the subtitle 'All and Everything'. In it he made use of the old legend that Beelzebub had been condemned by the Creator to expiate a fault committed in his youth by having to wander over an obscure and remote part of the universe, the solar system. Accompanied by his favourite grandson, Hassein, and an old servant, Ahoon, he makes a series of voyages in a space-ship and descends on to various planets of the solar system and at different periods of their history. It happens that his grandson is particularly interested in the queer behaviour of the inhabitants of the earth. 'What is the meaning,' he asks his grandfather, 'of the periodic outbreaks of reciprocal destruction amongst these strange earth-beings, the outbreaks that they themselves call by the name of war? What has gone wrong with their evolution so that their behaviour is unlike that of any other three-brained beings of our great universe?' His grandfather answers all these questions, and his answers, together with the accounts of Beelzebub's various descents on to the earth, permit of the author's giving a complete description of the tragic history of the human race. Gurdjieff's own description of this book is that it is 'An objectively impartial criticism of the life of Man.' His object in writing it is: 'To destroy, mercilessly, without any compromise whatsoever, in the mentation and feelings of the reader, the beliefs and views by centuries rooted in him about everything existing in the world.'

'How did Mr Gurdjieff fare during the German occupation?' I asked.

'He seems to have fared remarkably well.' A. answered. 'When it was obvious that Paris would fall, G.'s followers thought that he would be much better off in the country and they hurried him off to some suitable place. But these arrangements were not received very favourably by him and he bolted back to Paris in time to enter it with the German Army. He continued his work there in Paris during the whole of the occupation, but of course under considerable difficulties. Now he has a very vigorous Paris group, made up chiefly of young people, and he appears to think a lot of them. They work principally by means of the movements, and you will be able to see them doing their movements tomorrow afternoon at the Salle Pleyel.

A. looked at his watch and then said that we were expected at the flat in an hour's time. 'There will probably be a reading from one of his books,' he added. 'That will last about two hours, and then we shall all be invited to stay to lunch. I'd better tell you something about the meals there, because newcomers often find them rather difficult. Of course one soon gets used to them.'

'Why difficult?' we asked.

'Well, you see, there is an enormous amount to eat, and people from England seem to have lost their capacity to take proper meals. Then there is also the difficulty about the drink. You can choose armagnac, or red or white vodka, whichever you prefer.'

My wife reminded A. that I disliked alcohol and scarcely ever took any. 'He'll have to when he lunches or dines with Gurdjieff,' he replied. 'You see, he's a Russian and Russians always drink a lot of vodka. But there is another and far more important reason why all of G.'s guests have to drink, whatever happens to be their private tastes. A great many people are passing through his hands and he is compelled to *see* them as quickly as possible.' (A. emphasized the word 'see'.) 'Well, you know how alcohol opens up a man so that what he has previously managed to keep hidden is revealed. That is what the Arabs mean when they say that "alcohol makes a man more so".'

'What are G.'s rules?' I asked.

'There are a number of toasts to be drunk during the course of the meal and the usual rule is one glass of brandy or vodka for every three toasts. The women are let off with six toasts per glass.'

'How many toasts?' I inquired rather apprehensively.

'That varies, and it may be anything up to twenty-five.'

'Why all these toasts?' my wife asked. 'Whose health are we supposed to be drinking?'

'You know all about types,' A. began, and we nodded. 'Well, there is a whole science of types, a very ancient one supposed to have been developed in Babylon. We drink to the various types of men – there are twenty-three, I believe – coupled with the names of those who represent them. You'll be asked to select the type to which you belong.'

'Supposing one doesn't know it?'

'That doesn't matter. Just select the one that seems to suit you best. There's a director of ceremonies and you can let him know what sort of idiot you are.'

'Idiot?'

'Yes, he uses that word, but in its original and not in its acquired meaning. It really signifies "one's own" and it is therefore only another word for type. We had better settle with the waiter and get back to our hotel now, for we are due at the flat at twelve.'

Six or seven people were awaiting us in the hall of the Belfast Hotel and with these we made our way in a leisurely fashion down the Avenue Carnot. I already knew some of those with whom I was now walking, but others were strangers to me and I was told that they belonged to Mr Gurdjieff's American group. Rue des Colonels-Renard forms a cul-de-sac to the left of the Avenue Carnot, and it was in this street, in a typically Parisian block of flats, that Mr Gurdjieff lived. We entered the dark entrance hall of this building, walked up to the first floor and there A. knocked gently with his knuckles on the door. Somehow it seemed appropriate that entrance to Gurdjieff's abode should be gained by the more ancient system of knocking rather than by the peremptory modern method of ringing a bell. A knock was a more personal signal and did not necessarily imply that the visitor was confident that he would be admitted. The door was opened by a French girl of about seventeen, with strikingly dark eyes and a poise and maturity far beyond her years, who seemed to know most of those present. She let us into a tiny hall and disappeared without uttering a word. The hall was already crowded with people who had arrived before us and who were now waiting for a door on the right of the hall to be unlocked. This was the room in which the readings were always held, and Lise – this was the girl's name, I gathered – now reappeared with the key. As the hall emptied of people I was able to examine it better.

What a fantastic place it was. The strange mixture of furniture, the incongruous collection of pictures, the haphazard arrangement of the flat's contents gave it the appearance of a junk-shop rather than of a home. Everything seemed to have happened there by accident, and nothing by design. It was impossible to learn anything of the character of the owner from such a fortuitous collection of odds and ends. To the left of the hall was a passage and from this direction came muffled noises, as though someone were engaged in moving pots and pans about in a kitchen. Over the whole flat hung an unfamiliar odour that was neither English nor Parisian in character, but much more like the smell which pervades all Eastern bazaars. It made me think of Ceylon, and then suddenly I realized what it was – it was the smell of spices. The hall was so cluttered up with furniture that I had difficulty in finding a place in which to stow my overcoat. Finally I pushed it on to an already overburdened peg and followed the others into the room on the right.

It measured about fourteen feet square, and as the curtains of the windows were closely drawn, it was now lit only by artificial light. This sitting-room contained a divan, five or six chairs and a number of small wooden stools on which people were now perched like performing seals waiting for their turn to begin. On the left of the room there stood a large glass cabinet, the shelves of which were crowded with china ornaments, some of them valuable but too ornate to be beautiful. On the top of the cabinet there rested a huddle of dolls dressed in the various peasant costumes of Europe. The opposite corner of the room was occupied by a large structure of mirrors and gilt, a piece of furniture which a child would have adored. Everywhere on its many platforms of mirror could be seen gay little figures, men and women being drawn along in droskies, mounted soldiers, galloping Arab sheikhs, Nubians on camels, dancing ballerinas, everything that one could wish to find, and still more to be discovered, hidden away in some corner, after one had thought that one had seen them all. At present everything in this splendid world of gilt and mirrors was in semi-darkness, but if the wires were plugged in and the current switched on it would sparkle with dozens of tiny lights. Now it all looked a little forlorn and wistful, like a ballroom after a dance, or a banqueting-hall after the guests have departed. I had no time to examine anything more in the room for B. now entered with a sheaf of typewritten pages in his hand. He seated himself on a chair by the side of the divan, turned on a pedestal light, looked at us and then began to read.

During the reading the door leading out on to the hall occasionally opened to admit a late-comer, but an hour after the reading had begun my attention was distracted from it by the door being opened and held slightly ajar. Somebody was evidently looking into the room from the hall and was taking note of those present at the reading. Then, quietly and unobtrusively, Mr Gurdjieff entered the room and sat down on the vacant chair by the door. He was shorter and stouter than I had expected him to be but otherwise much as I had always pictured him, a man with dark piercing eyes and with a sweeping moustache now almost grey. No, he was not quite as I had pictured him, for the dark eyes were not piercing but lit with a friendly mirth. He made me think of that subject to be found in old Chinese paintings, the figure of the 'Old Rogue', the sage who has long ago discovered that men are not what they pretend to be, yet manages to like them all the same. It was laughter and not cynicism that lurked in our host's eyes and in the corners of his mouth as he sat there looking round at his guests.

The reading proceeded without interruption for another hour, but during that time my thoughts refused to follow the wanderings of Beelzebub any longer. They revolved instead around Beelzebub's creator, the old man sitting there on that chair only a few yards away from me. So this was Gurdjieff, who from his earliest youth had wandered over the least known parts of Asia searching for truth and determined to find it, the person to whom we owed the system. What interesting and thrilling things he would have to talk about if we could only induce him to speak of its discovery. Then, quite unexpectedly, Gurdjieff spoke, but of a subject much nearer home than the one in my mind. 'Le Patron,' he said, rubbing his hand over his rather prominent abdomen, 'is demanding instant attention, and le Patron is une personne trés importante, to be treated always with the greatest respect. He asks to be fed, and I invite you all to lunch.' Then he rose from his chair and left the room without any more words.

The small hall was again filled to overflowing so that it was almost impossible to move in it, but as I had heard my name being called, I made a special effort to force a way for myself and my wife through the crowd. We broke into the room opposite that in which we had recently been listening to the reading and Madame S. indicated to us that we should take our places at the far end of the long table. Mr Gurdjieff was already seated there, on a small divan, with one foot tucked comfortably under the other knee. We placed ourselves rather apologetically directly in front of him. More and more people continued to squeeze into the room, and those who failed to find a place at the main table sat at subsidiary tables, or else stood round with their backs propped up by the walls. It was astonishing how so many people could manage to find accommodation in such a small space. As all the guests were now well wedged into their places, the luncheon dishes were passed overhead by a human delivery belt, stretching from the kitchen to the head of the table. Within a few minutes the main dishes, covered by plates, were placed one on top of the other, to form a neat little pile in front of each guest.

Mr Gurdjieff now removed his *kalmak* with a natural gesture of dignity like that of a king renouncing his crown. A large bowl having been placed in front of him, he started to prepare a special treat for his guests. Into this bowl went chopped cucumber, pickles, red pepper, onions, fragments of bread, contributions from a number of different bottles containing various kinds of preserve, pieces of dried fish and finally large spoonfuls of sour cream. This mixture he carefully stirred and occasionally tasted, in the manner of an old apothecary preparing a specially potent elixir of life. It was not the type of dish to which I was accustomed, or one for which I had any instinctive liking, but I accepted my helping with as good a grace as possible.

The moment had now clearly come to begin eating, for the Master of Ceremonies had by this time made sure that every guest's glass was fully charged with armagnac or vodka. I dug out strange morsels from Gurdjieff's mixture with my spoon, and having transported them to my mouth was gratified to find that the cream had had an emollient effect on the more biting of its ingredients. Indeed, I could swallow them with comparative comfort. But how about the still more potent draught in the glass standing to the right of my place? Would the spoonfuls of cream I had scooped out of the bowl and swallowed be able to exorcize the fiery red devils which were so shortly to join them within the hallowed precincts of my stomach? I very much doubted it, but I made a plan that, when the time arrived – it could not be more than a few minutes ahead, for the Director of Ceremonies was now standing up – I would toss a third of that glass on to the back of my throat. It was in this manner that the Russians were reputed to drink, and who could know better than they how to dispose quickly of vodka? By now the Director had named the toast and, taking our time from Mr Gurdjieff, we swallowed our drinks and replaced our glasses on the table with a chorus of clatter. It was a fiery drink, but not quite so blistering as I had expected it to be. So far, so good. Now I would look at Mr Gurdjieff, separated from me only by the breadth of a narrow table and by a low fence of sauce bottles.

What an astonishing man he was, entirely different from anybody I had previously met. Now that the kalmak had been removed, the full splendour of his clean-shaven head was fully revealed. It rose to an immense height above the level of the ears, reaching its zenith at a point midway between the frontal region and the occiput. The next most remarkable feature about this head of his was that his face was completely devoid of wrinkles, although he claimed to be over eighty years of age. His olive-coloured face was smooth and serene, and at the same time charged with virile power, a face that recalled to me the Lohan figure which had made such a deep impression on me at the Chinese exhibition before the war. But at this stage of my study of Mr Gurdjieff's head, his eyes turned in my direction and he asked me whether it was true that I was a doctor. On hearing that this was so, he told me that he had always taken a great interest in medicine, and that he had practised the medical art in times of great emergency, such as when there had been a great outbreak of plague in China and of cholera in Persia.

'But why,' he suddenly asked, 'do you not eat more? Do you not like this kind of dish?'

'I like it very much, Mr Gurdjieff,' I answered, 'but I have just arrived from England and —'

'Ah, in England everyone starves! All English people who come to Paris act thus. They pick here and they pick there, like a sparrow' (he enacted a sparrow picking up crumbs) 'and they have quite lost the capacity to eat as a man should eat. It is sad, but they soon recover after a few days' treatment in Rue des Colonels-Renard.' Having delivered himself of this favourable prognosis, he smiled and handed me a special delicacy, a small fragment of smoked sturgeon. 'Now, M. le Directeur, the next toast, s'il vous plaît.' Mr Gurdjieff showed no partiality or exclusiveness in his use of the various languages and was prepared to throw into a single phrase as many different ingredients as he had recently thrown into his salad. Tonight he spoke in French, English and Russian, and what surprised me most was the fact that, although he could speak neither French nor English well, he was remarkably well-versed in the popular idiom of the day. This was particularly well illustrated by the remark he made to me a few minutes later. 'If you eat this and then drink some of that red vodka, for you it will be roses, roses all the way. But if you do one without the other, it will not be roses but only thorns.'

I kept reminding myself that I was sitting in a Parisian flat near to the Arc de Triomphe and that I was lunching with Mr Gurdjieff, but however often I repeated this sobering phrase to myself, I continually forgot that it was true. For me Paris was always becoming Baghdad, and Mr Gurdjieff was for ever changing places with Haroun-al-Raschid. Who but a Caliph could have managed to provide all these wonderful things to eat: pigeons stewed in vine leaves, pilaf, wild strawberries swimming in cream, wonderful sweetmeats, Turkish Delight, melons, avocado pears, everything that a greedy mind could imagine. It was quite true, as Mr Gurdjieff had just remarked, that everything would be roses, roses for me, but there still remained a very important obligation which I must not for a single moment forget. Until all these toasts were over, I must never relax my hold on that tiny place, deep within myself, which in spite of the behaviour of everything else, still stood firm and steady. It was now specially necessary for me to maintain this foothold, now that the table was swaying and that the old business of everything getting bigger and bigger and then smaller and smaller had begun. Mr Gurdjieff was behaving at this moment just as the gas-jet in my old nursery used to behave whenever I was kept in bed with a temperature. He would recede to an immense distance away and then, a minute later, come rushing forwards to meet me, till he eventually became so big that he completely swamped the room. Did this mean that I was back again in some feverish nursery dream from which I would shortly awake? No, this was no dream but a fragment of reality, something that was actually happening in this moment of time. I was at a luncheon party in the Rue des Colonels-Renard with Mr Gurdjieff, and Mary was here by my side, apparently quite undisturbed by all this drinking. But then women were such gifted actresses that one could never be quite sure what they were actually feeling. Appearances were so important to them that they had become artists in dissembling.

At long last the toasts came to an end, and when coffee in small bowls, accompanied by packets of cigarettes, appeared on the table, I suddenly felt as a shipwrecked sailor must surely feel when, after being buffeted about in a turbulent sea and all but drowned, he discovers that he has been cast up on to firm land in company with all his friends. It was all over and there was no need for me to drink anything more, and I could eat whatever I happened to like, and what could be more delectable than the large blob of Turkish delight that Mr Gurdjieff was now handing me. 'I invite you all to dinner tonight,' he said to the assembled company, 'and the reading will begin at half-past nine. Now I advise you to lie down and rest for a little, first on your left side and then on your right.' With these words the luncheon party closed.

Outside in the Rue des Colonels-Renard, the sun was shining and Parisians were going about their business and their pleasure with brisk movements and intelligent, friendly faces. I was surprised to find myself back again in daylight and I blinked in the sunshine like an owl that has made a grave error in the hour of his outing. It was not, as I had previously thought, early morning, but half-past three in the afternoon, and it would be wise therefore for us to return home to our hotel for a short rest before the beginning of the evening session.

'Well, what do you make of it all?' I asked of my wife after we had reached the haven of our room and had lain down on the bed fully dressed except for our shoes. 'What did you think of the flat?'

'Quite indescribable,' she answered. 'If anything was calculated to put you off and to convince you that everything in the Rue des Colonels-Renard was bogus, it was certainly that hall and those pictures.'

'And Mr Gurdjieff himself?'

There was a long pause. 'He's the most astonishing man I've ever met,' she said at last. 'The chief impression he gave me was one of immense vigour and of concentrated strength. I had the feeling that he was not really a man but a magician.'

'Of what variety?' I asked. 'Black or white?'

'I'm not quite sure, perhaps both, but at any rate, utterly ruthless.'

'I agree,' I answered, 'but under all that strength, behind all that ruthlessness of his, I saw a man with an immense compassion for mankind. He could be brutal and he could be cruel, but he would be cruel only as a surgeon is cruel when he operates. I also was conscious of his immense strength, but what struck me more forcibly than anything else was his essential kindness.'

'I think that you are probably right,' she answered, 'but he is a man who must always be treated with great care, for I believe that he could do almost anything that he really wanted to do with you.'

'Yes, he has immense power.'

'So much,' she answered, 'that to sit at table with him is like sitting near to a dynamo. He radiates strength.'

'What else can you say?' I asked.

'A lot, but I'm not going to say it yet. We've got to rest, for at half-past nine we are due back in Mr Gurdjieff's flat again. You've had a bit of tossing yourself with all that vodka, so I would advise you to try and get some sleep.'

I took what was obviously excellent advice.

CHAPTER XI

LIFE IN RUE DES
COLONELS-RENARD

IT would be fitting to insert here a picture of the man to whom everything recorded in the book is due – G. I. Gurdjieff. Fitting, yes, but as difficult a task as to paint a portrait of that old sea-god Proteus, 'who knew everything and was capable of assuming any shape'. Gurdjieff had Proteus' many-sidedness; he managed to combine in his person the qualities of a man and a woman, an angel and a devil, a mischievous boy and a dignified sage. He could create any impression he liked, and would often supply whatever his visitors expected of him. If they were looking for mystery, he gave them as much mystery as they needed; if they had been shocked by what they had previously heard about him, they were liable to leave his presence still more deeply shocked; if they believed him to be a charlatan, they had their disbelief confirmed. It was not part of his work to disarm hostility and to make converts, but to give help to those who had already discovered that they were in need of it.

Gurdjieff's ability to read men and to play any part that he deemed necessary was of great service to him in the past. When in 1917 he and his followers escaped from Russia, they had to pass through a countryside in a state of chaos. Detachments of the rival Red and White armies were hopelessly intermingled, so that it was impossible to foretell which party was in the ascendant in any given district. The only hope of getting through was to be on good terms with both, and this Gurdjieff achieved. By posing as a geologist who had discovered rich deposits of gold in the Caucasus, he obtained a loan of two lorries from the Bolsheviks, and by equally clever acting he secured permits to carry arms from both the Bolsheviks and from General Denikin's staff.

All that it is possible to do is to give the impressions which Gurdjieff created in me, and these can be summed up in the generalization that for me he represented the outcome of the work. By this I mean that he had achieved greater consciousness, control and unity than those possessed by other men. It is true that the consciousness of another person cannot be measured objectively, but the greater a man's consciousness, the more control he is able to exercise over his various functions. Everything Gurdjieff did seemed to originate from within. When he became angry, as he sometimes did, his anger had the appearance of being deliberate, and it was laid on one side as soon as it had served its purpose. The dark eyes would then regain their twinkle, the stern olive-coloured face would relax and the conversation would be resumed at the point at which it had been suddenly broken off. He never fumbled in his thoughts or his movements. The latter were always purposeful and made with the strictest economy of effort, like those of a cat, and his immense capacity for work was due to this ability of his never to waste energy. It was particularly noticeable that he had obtained complete mastery over his body. He had been involved in a serious motor accident shortly before our arrival in Paris and had been driven to a hospital in an ambulance with a broken sternum, various cuts on the head and many bruises. On the following day he discharged himself from the hospital, returned home and resumed his work. By watching him carefully I could see that certain movements caused him considerable pain, but he behaved as though he had fully recovered and insisted on his body obeying his commands, as always.

Within a short time I became accustomed to the unusual routine of the flat in Rue des Colonels-Renard, to lunching at the hour of two and dining after midnight. I was still conscious of the strange nature of my surroundings, of the unlovely pictures, of the drawn curtains and the artificial light, but they were no longer so obtrusive that they prevented me from seeing anything else. I realized now that whatever Gurdjieff did he did for some purpose, and that these lunches and dinners had not been arranged merely for the enjoyment of eating and drinking, but to bring us closer together and into more intimate relationship with him. Too much theorizing was tending to make the minds of his London followers too rigid and our behaviour too calculated and grim. We were in danger of acquiring the chapel-going faces of Plymouth Brethren, and we needed loosening up. If anyone was fitted to bring about this loosening process it was surely Gurdjieff, a man who had always lived life to its fullest, and, as some people thought, to excess. Under the excellent treatment meted out to us in the Rue des Colonels-Renard, our faces became relaxed and any puritanical trends rapidly disappeared. 'It is necessary,' Gurdjieff reminded us, 'to know when to be serious and when to laugh.' He said that sleeping man was without any proper standards; he was solemn when it was wiser to be gay, and he was frivolous when it was necessary to be serious. In other words, he had no idea of the true significance and value of the different things he encountered in his life.

There was yet another, to me very welcome, change which Gurdjieff was bringing about. Ouspensky was a strict disciplinarian, and, whenever any work had to be done for him, he had always issued detailed instructions exactly how it was to be carried out. Nothing was ever left to a pupil's discretion, and in the past so little encouragement had been given to initiative that, in some of us, enterprise was tending to atrophy. Personally, I always carried out Ouspensky's instructions as scrupulously as I could, but I had never on any account attempted to do any more. But with Gurdjieff I began to develop a sense of personal responsibility and to experience a new sense of freedom. At the same time it was a freedom which must be very carefully used, for the punishment for error was very great. It was the punishment of seeing one's teacher gravely inconvenienced by one's mistake; and it was difficult to be in close touch with Gurdjieff for long without developing an affection for him.

Beneath the daily routine of Rue des Colonels-Renard there ran an unobtrusive current of purpose, a current which would every now and then break through to the surface and reveal itself. This was particularly likely to happen when two or three of us were invited to take coffee with Mr Gurdjieff in his own private room. This sanctum was situated in the very heart of his flat, and it was actually the store-room from which emanated the odour of spices which always pervaded the hall. The walls of this room were traversed by tiers and tiers of wooden shelves all over-laden with every conceivable form of grocery; innumerable tins, packets of sweets, boxes of confectionery, bags of flour, oatmeal, currants, raisins and sugar, bottles of brandy and vodka. I am unable to think now of this room without a photographic image of it forming itself in my mind. The whole vivid scene comes back to me so that I look at it again in all its details. At a small table pressed up against a rampart of shelves mounting up to the ceiling sits Gurdjieff, with a large chocolate fish covered with shining tinfoil paper swinging just above the level of his immense head. Madame S. is seated there at his side ready to interpret for us difficult passages in his mixture of French, English and Russian, whilst the rest of us sit around him on small canvas-topped stools or upturned grocery boxes. Lise has deposited the tray of coffee bowls on the table, and Gurdjieff, after seeing that his guests' needs have been satisfied, fits his own cigarette with some difficulty – it is a little bit too big – into his holder. It is an occasion either for music or for a private talk, and we sit there sipping our coffee – the sugar must always be kept in the mouth and never be put into the bowl – and listening to his music or else to his words. If we have come here for music, Gurdjieff will have brought with him his special instrument, an unusual form of accordion. Balancing this on his knee, he presses backwards and forwards a hinged flap on the back of the accordion with his left hand and thereby obtains a rather spasmodic supply of air. His right hand rests on the keyboard, and, sometimes improvising and at other times remembering, he calls out of his instrument music of a kind that I have never listened to before. It is in a minor key and at one moment it calls back to my memory the song that the Mohammedan dockers at Suez chanted many years ago when our ship's coal bunkers were being replenished, and at other times it is more reminiscent of the mournful music I lis-tened to as a child as the sea surged backwards and forwards through the narrow entrance of a cave. Gurdjieff told us very little about the music he had collected during his travels, but it was obvious that it came from several sources. Some of it was clearly occupational in origin, songs sung by peasants while carrying on their crafts. There were, for example, the traditional songs chanted by the old carpet makers of Central Asia as they squatted on the floor of some large barn, combing, spinning and dyeing their wools or weaving them into well-known local patterns. Gurdjieff described how of a winter evening a whole village would take part in this work in which everybody had his allotted task to do, each with its own musical accompaniment. Another source from which he drew inspiration was the sacred music he had listened to in the various monasteries he had visited, monasteries of many kinds, Greek Orthodox, Essene and Sufi. I have little personal knowledge of music and can say only two things about what he played, first that it was very old and second that it had a strong emotional effect on most of his hearers.

If we had been invited to Gurdjieff's sanctum not for music but for a talk, the conversation was always of a very private nature. 'This that I tell you,' he would say, 'is for you alone and it must not be discussed with other people. I ask you to do this and then later, when you come next time to Paris, you can report to me what you find.' He would then outline some psychological or physiological exercise and give us very precise instructions how this exercise was to be carried out. While imparting these instructions he would speak with the exactitude of an old and experienced physician prescribing treatment to his patients, choosing his words very carefully and talking in grave and convincing tones. At such times his words fell on our ears with immense weight, for they seemed to be backed, not only by his own wisdom, but by the authority of a long line of unseen and unknown teachers. The message we had just received had come to us from a distance of thousands of years; it had been carefully passed on by word of mouth from a master to his disciple, who, in his turn, became a teacher charged with the special responsibility of passing on to others the traditional and ancient wisdom. For me, at any rate, Gurdjieff represented the last and visible link in an immensely long chain of teachers stretching back into a distant and misty past. How strange that the message should have reached me in such surroundings, amid bags of sugar and bottles of spices, packets of raisins and canned meats. But was it really so strange as I had at first taken it to be? It is well known that wisdom is to be found more often in the world's by-ways than in its lecture halls.

Two days after our arrival in Paris, the nature of the readings which always preceded the meals was changed. Instead of giving us chapters of his first book, *Beelzebub's Tales to His Grandson* to read, Gurdjieff supplied us with extracts from his second series of writings, *Meetings with Remarkable Men*. Who were these remarkable men whose lives he had taken such trouble to record in this second series of books? To answer this question a little more must be known about the earlier history of the author himself.

There is clear evidence that our host was not quite so old as he had made himself out to be, and everything points to his having been born in Alexandropol, near the Turkish frontier of Russia, on 1 January 1872. He came of Ionian-Greek stock, and his family had emigrated to the southern Caucasus in the year of the Turkish conquest of the Byzantine Empire. So it was in the Caucasian gateway to the vast continent of Asia that the young Gurdjieff was brought up, and there can be little doubt that his surroundings exerted a powerful influence on the development of his character. In more prosperous days his father had been the owner of large flocks of sheep and cattle, but he had lost all his possessions through the outbreak of some serious epidemic. After this disaster he adopted the profession of carpenter and moved with his family to Kars, a Russian military outpost a few miles from the Turkish frontier. Although poorly educated, in the sense in which this word is generally used, the elder Gurdjieff appears to have been a man of considerable attainments, and his son always referred to him with great respect. The elder Gurdjieff was not only a carpenter, but also an Asiatic bard who could recite by heart all the old legends and sagas that were chanted at village gatherings specially met together for this purpose. He was also keenly interested in religion and philosophy and counted amongst his friends many men who were far more highly educated than himself. These friends of his often came to the carpenter's workshop of an evening and the young Gurdjieff, seated on a pile of shavings in a corner of it, would listen to the philosophical and religious discussions of the grown-ups far into the night. These talks and the legends that his father recited had a great effect on the growing boy, and ultimately the influence they exerted on him became so strong that they altered the whole course of his life. That he was no ordinary boy is shown by the fact that the dean of the local cathedral – a great friend of his father – took upon himself full responsibility for his education. Dean Borsh would not allow him to be sent to the ordinary state school but arranged that he should be privately taught by men of his own choosing. His father readily agreed to this plan, and it was decided that the boy should eventually become both a priest and a doctor, it being impossible, in the opinion of the dean, to practise the one profession without at the same time practising the other.

The young Gurdjieff showed a great interest in science, and it was no hardship for him to have to study the subjects preliminary to his course in medicine. It would indeed have been difficult to name any subject in which the boy was not keenly interested, and the danger which threatened him was that his energies would become dissipated over too wide a field. Unwittingly his father increased this risk. 'The great thing in education,' he declared, 'was not to accumulate a vast store of information but to learn how to learn.' In order to teach his own son how to learn he adopted a certain procedure. The boy was set a certain piece of work to do with his hands, and as soon as he had discovered the right technique for doing it, this work was immediately stopped and another entirely different type of work begun. By this means the young Gurdjieff rapidly learnt a number of trades, and what was of greater importance, how to learn.

But the outside interest which finally brought his medico-priestly education to an end was not the learning of too many crafts but a growing curiosity concerning the nature of the inexplicable events that were happening around him. Strange people wandered with their flocks over the broad grazing grounds of the Caucasus, and none more curious than the Yezidis, or Devil-Worshippers. This tribe had incomprehensible customs, and their lives seemed to be bound by laws that exerted no influence over other races. It was, for instance, no uncommon sight to see what he had more than once witnessed, a Yezidi boy completely incapable of stepping outside a circle which somebody had drawn around him. How could the strange fact be explained that, until the circle had been erased, the boy was held a prisoner? And there were many other mysteries besides this on which science could throw no light.

Gurdjieff had always listened to his father's recital of ancient Assyrian and Sumerian legends with intense interest, and he now began to ponder over these old stories more and more. He believed that they contained hidden meanings which people had once known but had now lost. If he could only find the key to their symbolism, he would recover valuable knowledge now long forgotten. Eventually the young Gurdjieff's interest in the inexplicable and the very old took precedence over everything else. His attention turned more and more in the direction of the past, and he spent much of his time on archaeological research and in the study of ancient history. The career that had been mapped out for him was abandoned, and for the rest of his life he devoted himself to the single aim of searching for Ancient Knowledge.

We next find Gurdjieff acting as the leading spirit of a society formed under the title of 'Seekers of the Truth'. It was an association of young men who devoted themselves to the quest for esoteric knowledge, a search which took them into all the neighbouring countries, Persia, Turkestan and Afghanistan. As the years passed the Seekers were joined by men of maturer years endowed with a greater abundance of worldly goods. Not that shortage of money would seem to have been a serious handicap to Gurdjieff's previous search for truth. He had showed a wonderful capacity for replenishing the society's treasury with funds whenever it was empty, earning money in a score of different ways: by the manufacture and sale of plaster figures or artificial flowers, by a travelling workshop for the repair of household breakages, by the purchase and resale of rugs, and by other forms of trading. But the influx of more influential and better endowed men into the society allowed of more ambitious journeys being undertaken and the Seekers now extended their search into Tibet, the borders of India, China and even as far afield as Egypt, the Indonesian Archipelago and Australia. Disguised perhaps as Mohammedan pilgrims or Assyrian traders they reached remote regions of Asia which few Europeans had ever explored, became inmates of old-world brotherhoods and, after enduring many hardships, at last discovered what they had long been looking for, an orally transmitted knowledge not to be found in books. By putting all their new knowledge together, and by linking it up with what they had previously learnt from modern science, they constructed a self-consistent system of knowledge, afterwards to become known to us as 'the system'. The remarkable men of whom Gurdjieff had written in his second series of books were the men who had helped him in all his work.

Whatever may have been Gurdjieff's personal desires after the search was over, he believed it to be his duty to return to Europe and to teach the West what he had learnt in the East. He therefore made his way back to Moscow where he purchased an estate with the intention of creating an Institute for the Harmonious Development of Man. But World War I prevented the further development of his plans. It was in this year, 1915, that Ouspensky met him while visiting Moscow. Although originally prejudiced against Gurdjieff by a rather flamboyant notice appearing in the press about a ballet which Gurdjieff had written and intended to produce, 'The Struggle of the Magicians', Ouspensky was so deeply impressed by Gurdjieff himself that he abandoned his own work in order to join his group. He was one of that small band of followers that, under the leadership of Gurdjieff, made its way through the chaos of the Russian Revolution to Constantinople.

The more I saw of Gurdjieff the more convinced I became of his uniqueness. He had qualities which I had never seen in any-body else; profound knowledge, immense vitality and complete immunity from fear. He was old but was still capable of working for a longer time than anybody else.

Few people realized how busy he was between our visits to the Rue des Colonels-Renard. Not only had he his French followers to look after but there was a number of indigent Russian refugees to be fed in his flat. Many a person in trouble made his way to the Rue des Colonels-Renard for help and advice, for Gurdjieff was a familiar figure to the frequenters of the neighbouring cafés.

I now understood Gurdjieff better, but this did not mean that I was no longer puzzled by what he sometimes did and said. What, I often asked myself, do these contradictions, these floutings of social conventions mean? Why must we be submitted to these shocks? At times I was seriously disturbed and sought in vain for an explanation of what had happened. He was a genius and a genius is often erratic When Nature endows an individual with special gifts, she often adjusts the balance by subtracting something from him which ordinary men possess. Was this the explanation of Gurdjieff's eccentric behaviour? No, it was not, for this was no oversight on Gurdjieff's part, but deliberate policy.

His offences, as a writer, against literary conventions were as obvious as were his offences, as a man, against social customs. At first I was inclined to attribute this to inexperience, for he had never had any desire to be an author. The writing of books had been forced upon him, and it was absurd therefore to demand of him subservience to literary rules. But a few days after I had accepted this explanation I was forced to discard it. When readings from his second book began I was immediately struck by the change in the author's literary style. His portraits of the companions who had accompanied him in his journeys were works of art. So skilfully were their characters drawn that they became for me living and likeable men whom I had met in some distant and all but forgotten past. Here in this book was excellent writing, descriptions of people and scenery which showed great literary ability. Here was a book I would have been proud to have written, a book which, if it were ever to be published, would be widely read. But even this book had been spoilt by what I felt to be lapses of taste. It was as though every now and then a mischievous imp had jumped out of the inkpot, scurried over the paper and deliberately ruined the beauty of all that had been written. 'Oh, why,' I would inwardly protest as I listened to the reading, 'why has he suddenly dropped from that high level of writing and inserted that utterly trivial remark?' Nor was this all for which the accursed ink-bottle imp had been responsible; his escapades had not only ruined the literary merit of the book, but had thrown doubt on the veracity of its contents. There could be no doubt that Gurdjieff had visited most of the places he so vividly described, and that the events and conversations he recorded had actually taken place. Yet sometimes happenings were included which I was quite unable to accept as true. And as I listened to this new affront to my credulity, I again became aware of that inner sense of grievance, of that clamour of protesting voices, of that insistent 'Why?' rising up in my mind and demanding an answer.

And suddenly the answer came to me. All this that puzzled me in Gurdjieff's behaviour and in his writing, like many things that he did, served a purpose. This emotional disturbance in me, this inner discord, this shouting within me of contradictory voices, this incessant struggle between 'Yes' and 'No', all this was deliberately provoked, both as a test and as a form of treatment. Gurdjieff's function was not to quieten but to disturb one. As a physician sometimes induces a violent reaction in his patient's body, so Gurdjieff deliberately provoked a violent reaction in his followers' souls. 'Shock therapy' is used in the treatment of diseases which have become chronic and to which the body no longer offers any resistance. The more I thought about this analogy between the physician's treatment of the indifferent body and Gurdjieff's treatment of the indifferent soul, the better it seemed to explain all that had previously puzzled and disturbed me.

I had long overstayed my leave and letters and telegrams were now arriving daily summoning me back to England. Part of me wanted to remain in Paris, but I was aware of a cleft in my feelings. There was another part of me which welcomed the fact that professional duties made it imperative that I should return to London. I had gained much from my visit to Paris and from my talks with Gurdjieff, but I longed for a simple and more customary mode of living. It was not that vodka was a trial to me, for I had found a means of consuming less of the fiery drink, and if Gurdjieff noticed this – few things escaped him – he had made no comment. Nor did my conscience prick me for having conspired to reduce my alcoholic intake. For several meals I had sat there at the end of that long table spiritually naked and vodka was no longer needed to prize open the hard shell of my personality. No, it was not escape from the fieriness of vodka and armagnac which my wife and I now sought but the resumption of a simpler and, to us, more natural form of life. We both longed to be at our cottage again, to work there in the garden and to talk with simple country neighbours. I had a strong desire to discuss with the local farmer the problem of obtaining better grass in the further meadow and to get his advice about re-draining it and wiring it against rabbits. In fantasy I saw myself inspecting the ditches and then passing through the little hunting gate into the woods to regain the cottage by the usual detour. I felt that I had had a surfeit of crowded cities, of drawn curtains and artificial light, of heavy meals, of slumbering by day and of struggling to keep awake at night. Above all, I wanted time to think about everything and to extract from it whatever I could. In short there was a large part of me which was pleased with this prospect of soon returning home.

Nevertheless it was with a certain feeling of disquiet faintly tinged with guilt that I made my way for the last time to Rue des Colonels-Renard, entered the dark hall, climbed the stairs and knocked at Gurdjieff's door. All these surroundings, which at first had seemed so utterly strange, were by now becoming familiar and even ordinary. No, not ordinary, for when I stepped into

Gurdjieff's hall the transition from the outside world of Paris to the inside world of the work was just as abrupt as it had always been. Here in this flat everything was extraordinary and paradoxical. It was extraordinary and yet at the same time it was far more real than the conventional world which lay without.

On hearing that I was shortly to leave, Gurdjieff invited me to his private room. Again we sat drinking coffee and smoking cigarettes whilst I watched him – fascinated as always – with the blue tinfoil-covered fish dangling over his head. On the table between us there reposed no only coffee and ashtrays but a bottle of vodka placed on top of a large tin of guava jelly.

'They tell me you go today,' he began.

'I'm afraid it can be postponed no longer,' I replied. 'Thank you very much for all —'

He waved my unfinished remark aside. 'Come again,' he said, 'whenever you like. This is your home and I shall always bid you welcome to it. Here I have for you a small present.' He pointed to the tin with its superimposed bottle. 'You take one and with it you take the other. It will last a week. I will make special arrangements to send you a fresh supply every week by somebody travelling to England.'

Vodka? Was he laughing deep inside himself and answering the laughter which lay equally well interred within myself? Or was it only his routine method of expressing his hospitality that had dictated the selection of these two gifts? I shall never know. What I did know, at that moment, was that a bond had been formed between me and this wonderful old man which I, for my part, would never seek to break. Could I indeed break it if I were to try? I very much doubted this, for I was surprised at the warmth of feeling which swept over me as I took his hand, bade him goodbye and closed the door quietly behind me.

CHAPTER XII

HE WAS A MAN

NEWS reached me in London that Mr Gurdjieff was leaving soon for America to visit his American groups and to arrange for the publication of his first series of books. I decided to go and see him again before he sailed. It was an inconvenient moment to leave London – when, indeed, is it other than inconvenient to break a routine? – but something told me that I must go. Mr Gurdjieff was now old and it was rumoured that during the last few weeks he had not been well. There was no saying how much longer he would be with us, this extraordinary man who had been our teacher for more than a quarter of a century. Yes, a quarter of a century, for even although we had known him only a few months, it was to him that we really owed everything we had learnt from Ouspensky. I booked a return ticket to Paris and two days later left London.

Nothing had changed in the Rue des Colonels-Renard since I was last there except that the hall had shrunk still further owing to the presence in it of some enormous trunks already packed for the coming voyage. I gathered that Gurdjieff managed to reproduce in his New York hotel room, a very passable replica of the Rue des Colonels-Renard ménage, and this meant his taking with him a great deal of equipment. It was his custom to invite large crowds to his New York hotel room, to cook the usual large meals over a small stove in his bathroom and to entertain his guests far into the night. It was not surprising therefore that the trunks, amongst the largest I have ever seen, blocked half of the hall. He gave me a warm welcome back to Paris and, after the usual reading, invited me to sit near to him again. I felt unexpectedly at home now in a room in which I had not always been at my ease. However much Mr Gurdjieff might disturb one – and it was his function to do this – he certainly had the secret of eliciting the affection of his pupils. No longer handicapped by having to struggle with an overdose of vodka, or having to eat more than I required, I could observe him and his methods of teaching more closely. As I sat there watching his gestures and listening to his forcible words, I was carried straight back to the old days of the house at Hayes and to Madame Ouspensky at her best. It was from Gurdjieff that she had culled many of her telling phrases, and from him that she had learnt to see in different men and women various kinds of animals. 'You are a turkey-cock,' he said to someone on the first evening, 'a turkey-cock pretending to be a real peacock.' A few masterly movements of his head, a guttural sound or two and there appeared at the table an arrogant gobbler parading itself before a hen. A little later a much larger animal materialized before our eyes. 'Why do you look at me as one kind of bull looks at another kind of bull?' he asked of someone else. And with a slight change in the expression of his eyes, in the carriage of his head and in the curve of his mouth, a challenging bull was produced for our inspection. During his travels, whenever money ran short, as it frequently did, Mr Gurdjieff earned it in a great many different ways. Had he wished to do so he could easily have added to his repertory the role of public entertainer.

The company was smaller than usual, and that evening the talk became more intimate, as though we were no longer looked upon as guests but as members of his family. He spoke of a visit on the morrow to a certain château situated some thirty kilometres from Paris, a château that it might be advisable for him to buy. He said that work would begin on a much larger scale after his return from the United States and that more accommodation would be needed. We London visitors could then be put up at the château instead of having to stay at hotels. Gurdjieff announced that there would be two cars available for transport tomorrow and that he would take with him as many people as possible, but of course some of us would have to be left behind. These unfortunates would receive compensation for not being included in the party by receiving presents afterwards from those who had been able to go. This would be obligatory to all taking part in the expedition. I write of this expedition not because it was of any particular importance – he often arranged excursions for us – but because it illustrates one of Gurdjieff's methods of revealing people to themselves. He deliberately created a background against which personalities were projected like shadows thrown on to a brightly lit screen. By doing this there was no need for him to call their attention to what he had noticed for they could see it clearly themselves. I took no part in the excursion, having something to do in Paris, but I was present when the excursionists returned. 'Now,' said Gurdjieff, 'we will make amends to the less fortunate by giving them their presents.' A feeling of awkwardness and tension could be felt in the room, and then someone explained that the expedition had been made on a Sunday, that all the shops had been shut, that the cars had started back as soon as the tour of the château had been completed, in short that there had been no chance of buying anything. Gurdjieff drew from behind him a number of paper packets and boxes and handed them round. He said very little, but it was realized that there are ways in France of buying things even on a Sunday, provided that one is sufficiently persistent and has not forgotten the promise made to those who have been left behind.

My visit to Paris was this time only a short one, its main purpose being to allow me to say goodbye to Mr Gurdjieff. His thoughts were obviously directed to the coming publication of his book. It would appear, he said, first in America and then, a few months later, it would be published in England, France and Germany. He expected that many people would misunderstand what he had written, and men and women would be needed to expound its meaning to others. He said that he had spare copies of his manuscript and that he would let me have one to take back to London, where it could be read at meetings. Time was short, he said, and there was much to be done, for who knew what would happen to mankind in the coming years? As he spoke we detected in his voice and in his words a note of urgency as though he were engaged in a struggle with the 'merciless Heropass', to whom he refers so often in his writings – the swift passage of the years.

We asked him about the future of the work in London and he replied that he would think about paying us a visit after he had returned from the States. In any case, he would give us all possible help by sending us one of his best French experts in the movements. Classes in the special exercises would then be started in London. The young Frenchman he proposed to send us was at present in New York preparing for his own visit there, but he would be free to come to England as soon as they all returned. We said goodbye to him in his room, leaving him there at his tiny table smoking his cigarette and deep in thought. I was conscious of a change in him, a deterioration in his health; there was a bluish tinge about his lips, his breathing was more rapid and his ankles appeared to me to be swollen. But his body had always been forced to obey his commands, and he still compelled it to do all that he required of it. The pressure of his work had not been reduced; if anything it had been increased by his coming visit to America.

When one looks back and recalls the inexorable march of events, one is tempted to invest them with a significance that at the moment of their happening they were not seen to possess. Writing as I now do of my meetings with Gurdjieff, both before and after his return from America, I seem to see in them presages of his approaching death. Did I look upon these events as omens at the time, or is it only now that I invest them with this meaning? I do not know. The only thing of which I can be sure is that his health gave rise to a growing anxiety in our minds, an anxiety which forced us to realize that, despite his vigour, we could not count on his being with us for very long.

One of the most striking features of these last reunions in Rue des Colonels-Renard was the number of young people who crowded round his table, especially after his return from America. Those of his followers who were parents seemed to have realized that the moment had come for taking their children to Paris. They might understand very little, but they wanted them to be able to recall in later years having, a long time ago, met a very remarkable man in France, a certain Mr Gurdjieff. To ensure their being able to do this, children ranging in age from three to fourteen were now being brought to Paris and invited to the flat in Rue des Colonels-Renard. There they sat at his table warmly welcomed and specially entertained by him. He had the simplicity of a great man, and he enjoyed their presence at his table, loading them with presents and sometime causing their parents embarrassment by the amount of food he pressed on them. Some of the children were shy, but most of them were at their ease, laughing at his jokes and promptly replying to his questions. For him, very young people were of far greater importance than the rest of us, for they were representatives of a future generation of men and women, a generation which had not yet been ruined and which, by right teaching and upbringing, might possibly be saved. I like to remember these youthful gatherings, for when I look back on them I recall not only the children, but Gurdjieff in a new role, Gurdjieff as grandfather, dispenser of gifts and enjoyer of fun.

During this visit to Paris on the eve of Gurdjieff's departure for America, I realized that the relationship Gurdjieff established with his followers might be intimate, but that it was always an impersonal one. He would storm at one or other of us, with an anger which it was frightening to witness, but when it was all over no irritating sting would be left behind. He had attacked self-love and deceit in general wherever it happened to manifest itself, and on this occasion it had happened to make its appearance in Mr A. or Miss B. or Mrs C. It was not with A. as an individual that he had been angry, but with his action in allowing poison from him to pollute the room. Nor was it necessary that A. should have spoken to call forth a reprimand, for he had an uncanny ability to diagnose our inner state without a word having been uttered. I recall a meal at which I caught an observation he made in a low voice to his senior follower in the room, an observation that was not intended for my ears. 'Heavy vibrations coming from the other end of the table, J.' So, also, when he displayed affection, it was not because he had a partiality for that particular person, but because he had an all-embracing affection for everything that was real. Having become aware of something genuine and lovable stirring in one of those present, he had accorded it an affectionate welcome. That Gurdjieff believed that the ability of a man to be impartial in his affections was of great importance to his development is clearly brought out in his writings. Thus he made his saintly character, Ashiata Shiemash, speak on the eve of his mission to the earth as follows: 'When I completed my seventeenth year, I began, as commanded from Above, to prepare my planetary body in order, during my responsible existence "to be able to be" impartial' (p. 353–4). And again: 'But never do beings-men here (on the planet earth) love with genuine impartial and non-egoistic love' (p. 358).

The summer of 1949 was a particularly fine one, and several motoring tours to Switzerland and to various parts of France were arranged. Gurdjieff had followers scattered all over France whom he occasionally visited, and there were also business affairs to be attended to. He welcomed these excuses for leaving Paris and for motoring along the long straight roads bordered by trees, with one or two cars following in his wake. His health also seemed to benefit from these outings, and especially from taking the baths at Vichy. He paid several visits to this health resort, and whenever he did so, he insisted that those who accompanied him there should also experience the health-giving qualities of the baths.

It required no expert medical knowledge to see that in spite of his good spirits and unflagging vigour his health was deteriorating. His breathing was still more laboured, and the tinge of blueness I had previously noticed had deepened. There were several doctors amongst his French and Russian followers who were said to be looking after him. Sitting near to him as I did at meals, I noticed that he ate and drank less. This was all to the good but was this everything that the medical profession could manage to do to prolong his life? It was obvious that he was suffering from ascites and that the fluid in his abdomen had increased to such an extent as to embarrass the work of the lungs, the heart and the digestive system. I made up my mind to take the first possible opportunity of speaking to him privately about his health, however much he might resent my interference.

My chance came when I went into his private room to say goodbye to him. I had been warned that he had previously dismissed a doctor who had expressed an unsolicited medical opinion about his health with the words, 'You may be a very clever doctor, but you are also a very big fool,' but I was prepared to take all risks. I told him that I was not his medical adviser but that I could not help looking at him through professional eyes. These eyes had told me that he was far from well; his breathing was difficult, his lips were blue and his ankles were swollen. His girth had also increased, and I believed that there was a great deal of fluid in his abdomen. By pressing on the diaphragm, this embarrassed his breathing. If this were true, as I believed it to be, it was obvious that the fluid should be removed as soon as possible by puncture. To do this would not entail anything that could be called an operation, but it would mean his going into a nursing home or hospital for at least a week. He listened carefully to what I had to say, nodding his head from time to time to indicate that he understood. Then, when I had finished, he replied: 'Yes, my doctors have told me that I have fluid but we await the arrival by plane of a new drug from America. We shall try this medical treatment first, and if it fails I will do what you say. Thank you for your advice.'

'But please, Mr Gurdjieff, let there be a time limit to purely medical treatment. Don't wait too long, for I believe that more radical measures are now badly needed.'

He promised not to delay if the new drug he was daily expecting proved unsuccessful. I took my leave of him and closed behind me the door of that strange room with its medley of odours, its tins, bottles and packages from all over the world, and with its blue fish dangling from a nail just above his head. Little did I realize that I would never re-enter it or speak again to the man for whom I had such a respect and, as I now discovered, affection.

Ten days later news came that much had happened since I had left. One of Mr Gurdjieff's followers in America, a New York physician, had flown over to Paris and had swept him into the American Hospital there. He was in the hospital at that moment having treatment, including abdominal puncture. Then a staccato series of telephone messages arrived in London with startling rapidity. The puncture had been carried out and he was much relieved; a complication had arisen and his condition had suddenly become grave; he was sinking; he was dead.

Gurdjieff dead! It was difficult to believe that all that vigour, that daemonic force, that keen intelligence, those unique qualities, no longer existed. Gurdjieff had always arranged and controlled everything he did, and one was tempted to wonder whether he had not contrived also this, his own death, in order to further some purpose connected with the work. Perhaps he was giving us a shock for the good of our souls, and then, when this had produced its effect, he, our teacher, would reappear, more vital even than before. It was impossible to connect Gurdjieff with the apathy and unresponsiveness of death. He stood for life, vigour, intelligence and action and I could not associate him with anything else.

He was buried in accordance with the ritual and customs of the Greek Orthodox Church, and for four days and nights his body lay in state in a small chapel within the grounds of the American Hospital. People came from all over Europe to gaze at him for the last time, and some even flew to Paris from America. At every hour of the day and night the tiny chapel was filled to overflowing with watchers and mourners, and never have I seen at any funeral such genuine grief. However much he may have sinned against the conventional code of morality, and sinned he certainly had, there could be no doubt of the devotion he had inspired.

As I sat there in that tiny chapel I tried to think of everything he had told me, and particularly of anything he had written or said on the subject of death. Death was for him 'the sacred rascooarno', an inevitable rite to which all must bend the knee, an abrupt ending of one thing and maybe a beginning of another. For death every man must prepare during his life. And the words of a toast came into my mind, a toast I had often drunk sitting beside him. 'To all those who are *candidates for an honourable death*, and to the health of those who are *candidates for perishing like dogs.*' I heard again the emphasis he placed on these two endings in order to bring out their difference, and I could see him looking gravely round the table to make sure that we had all understood the import of the toast and the need to prepare for an honourable death. Well, if any man had been a candidate for an honourable death, it was surely he, for no man had struggled more valiantly to carry out his obligations and to convert his five inherited talents into ten. The demands he made of others were as nothing in comparison with the demands he had always made of himself. Our efforts were but feeble gestures compared with his.

Everything in Gurdjieff was on a big scale, what one disliked in him as well as what one liked. He provoked strong reactions in everybody who came into contact with him, and it was part of his policy to provoke such reactions. There were two touchstones to character of which he made special use, a man's reactions to money and to sexuality, and it is not surprising that the resentments he aroused in his victims in connection with these two tests led to the belief that he was without moral principles. He required a great deal of money for his work and for the support of his numerous dependants. People, he said, only valued what they had paid for, and he had no hesitation in extracting from his followers as much as, or often more than, they could afford. This painful process of reducing bank balances was always referred to as 'shearing' and was accompanied by much badinage and mirth. Money poured out of his pocket as quickly as it entered it, for he was princely in his gifts. He would pay the expenses of people who were insufficiently well off to come to Paris to see him and support others of his followers who had fallen on bad times. He was well acquainted with poverty, and although little attempt was made to reduce the cost of his entertaining in his flat – to some of us it seemed unnecessarily extravagant – he spent comparatively little on himself. Money was of no interest to him except as a means to the carrying on of his work.

The key to the understanding of much that has been misunderstood in him is undoubtedly supplied by a study of his book *Beelzebub's Talks to His Grandson*, now published under the title *All and Everything*. First novels are usually autobiographical, and although *All and Everything* is not a novel but an allegory, it contains much that throws light on its author. The chief character in this allegory, Beelzebub, was born in the far distant planet of Karatas, and he was fashioned in a form quite different from that of a man, possessing hooves, a tail and, until he was deprived of them as a punishment, horns. Yet as one continues to read, the description of Beelzebub slowly fades, however one struggles to retain it, and the picture of a human being with an immense head, a sweeping moustache and dark observant eyes takes its place. Instead of watching Beelzebub travelling through the geography and history of this earth, one can only see the wanderings of Gurdjieff. It is Gurdjieff whom one espies sitting at 'Chaihanas' sipping tea with some fellow traveller and discussing with him the strange ways of men. It is Gurdjieff who descends on to the earth at the time of the Babylonian civilization to attend the debates between the great scholars of the day as to whether man has or has not a soul. The author of the book is always proving too strong for his own characters and is continually speaking instead of them and edging them off the stage. So when Beelzebub replies to a question of his grandson about the difference between right and wrong, it is Gurdjieff and not Beelzebub who is speaking.

'And which of these manifestations,' asks Hassein, 'do they [the earth beings] consider good and which bad?'(p.342). His grandfather answers that there are two independent understandings on the earth concerning right and wrong. 'The first of these understandings,' he says, 'exists there under the following formulation: Every action of man is good, in the objective sense, if it is done according to his conscience, and every action is bad, if from it later he experiences remorse' (p. 342). Beelzebub then explains to his grandson that there is a second earthly understanding of right and wrong, which, 'passing from generation to generation through ordinary beings there, gradually spread over almost the whole planet under the name of morality.'(p. 342). Beelzebub evidently thinks very poorly of this morality for he adds that its distinguishing mark is that it has the 'unique property which belongs to the being bearing the name chameleon' (p. 343).

Mr Gurdjieff always laid great stress on conscience and he develops this theme very fully in the chapter of his book in which he describes the arrival on the earth of a Divine Messenger, Ashieta Shiemash, sent from Above on a mission to man. He recounts how the saintly Ashieta Shiemash, during a preliminary period of fasting, ponders over the best method of discharging his mission and comes to the conclusion that it is useless for him to appeal to the ideas of which his predecessors have always made use, Faith, Hope and Charity. It is useless because the mentation of men has degenerated so badly that they are no longer able to grasp the true meaning of these sacred 'being-impulses', Faith, Hope and Charity. He decides therefore to appeal to something else that has not entirely atrophied in them – their consciences. 'Thanks to the abnormally established conditions of external ordinary being-existence existing here [on the earth], this factor [conscience] has gradually penetrated and become embedded in that consciousness which is here called "subconsciousness", in consequence of which it takes no part whatever in the functioning of their ordinary consciousness' (p. 359). Ashieta Shiemash decides to try to awake this submerged and quiescent conscience in the hope that it can be made to participate 'in the general functioning of that consciousness of theirs in which they pass their daily, as they say, "waking existence"' (p. 359). By this means he may be able to bring about the salvation of mankind. The chapter concludes with a description of the successful discharge of this mission and with an account of the period of peace and goodwill on earth which followed it.

There were two other words, besides conscience, of which Gurdjieff made constant use, the words duty and responsibility. He said that on arriving at a certain age every man had certain duties to perform; he must justify his existence by service to his fellow creatures and to his Creator. A child was exempt from duties and responsibilities but on attaining manhood he must learn to discharge faithfully both of these obligations. In an early chapter of his book he recounts how the young Hassein was overcome 'with a sense of indebtedness' to those who in the past, through their labours and their sufferings, have brought about the conditions which he, as a newcomer, enjoys. His grandfather replies that he does not as yet have to repay this debt.

> The time of your present age is not given you in which to pay for your existence, but for preparing yourself for the future, for the obligations becoming to a responsible three-brained being.
>
> So in the meantime, exist as you exist. Only do not forget one thing, namely, at your age it is indispensably necessary that every day, at sunrise, while watching the reflection of its splendour, you bring about a contact between your consciousness and the various unconscious parts of your general presence. Try to make this state last and to convince the unconscious parts – as if they were conscious – that if they hinder your general functioning, they, in the period of your responsible age, not only cannot fulfil the good that befits them, but your general presence, of which they are part, will not be able to be a good servant of our *Common Endless Creator* and by that will not even be worthy to pay for your arising and existence. (p. 78)

It was not only in his writings that Mr Gurdjieff stressed the importance of the obligation which the mature man must faithfully discharge. I recall very vividly an evening on which he inquired my age, and, having learnt that I was the oldest person present, except himself, he turned to the others and said: 'You notice that I do not treat everybody in the same way. I treat seniority with respect and so also must you.' Then, speaking directly to me, he added: 'And you on your part must discharge your responsibilities as an older person. When people apply to you for help you must give them what they expect of you, for you also have to make payment. Always bear in mind that every age has its appropriate duty to perform.' It was indeed a general principle of the work that the more senior the standing of the member of the group, the more was expected of him; a lapse that could be pardoned in another person could not be pardoned in him; an effort that was sufficient elsewhere was not sufficient for him. All manifestations of personality and of self-love in an older person were received with a special scorn.

And it was with man's personality that Gurdjieff was always at war, for it was this that prevented his making contact with the deeper and more real parts of his being. It is on this note that his book *All and Everything* begins and on this note that it closes. In the last chapter he recounts how Beelzebub, having completed his mission, returns triumphantly home. As the space-ship is nearing its destination his grandson puts a final question to him. 'How would you answer,' he asks, 'if God were to summon you into His presence and inquire of you what means could be adopted to save the inhabitants of the earth?' To this question Beelzebub replies:

> The sole means now for the saving of the beings of the planet Earth would be to implant again into their presences a new organ ... of such properties that every one of these unfortunates, during the process of existence, should constantly sense and be cognizant of the inevitability of his own death as well as of the death of everyone upon whom his eyes or his attention rests.
>
> Only such a sensation and such a cognizance can now destroy the egoism completely crystallized in them that has swallowed up the whole of their Essence and also that tendency to hate others which flows from it – the tendency, namely, which engenders all those mutual relationships existing there, which serve as the chief cause of all their abnormalities unbecoming to three-brained beings and maleficent for them themselves and for the whole of the Universe (p 1183).

I am convinced that Gurdjieff followed the dictates of his con-science and that when he sinned he sinned only against the moral code which 'has the unique property which belongs to the being bearing the name of chameleon'. When he offended conventional morality he did so openly, for no person cared less for his own reputation than he. If told that somebody had criticized him adversely for something he had done, he would laugh and say that this was as nothing compared with what some people thought and said of him.

As I looked at him for the last time and thought of all he had achieved in the course of his long life and how much I owed him, the oddities in his behaviour which in the past had puzzled and even troubled me were forgotten. What trifles they became when viewed in relationship to the whole man. What Hamlet had said of his father, the dead king of Denmark, I could truly say of him,

He was a man. Take him for all in all,
I shall not look upon his like again.
(I,ii,187-8)

CHAPTER XIII

THE SOURCE OF GURDJIEFF'S KNOWLEDGE

THIS record of a journey in a realm of ideas now ends. I am conscious of the insufficiency of my account of the system, but it was never my intention to expound more fully Gurdjieff's teaching. This has already been done, and with a masterly clarity, by Ouspensky, in his book *In Search of the Miraculous*. Gurdjieff's system of thought is also to be found by those who have the diligence to search for it in his own work, *All and Everything*. My object in writing this book was not to give an account of a special method of development, which, to be effective, requires oral and individual tuition, but to describe the impact of these ideas upon myself. Having achieved this limited project two questions only remain to be considered, the validity of Gurdjieff's system of knowledge and the source from which he obtained it. To neither of these questions can a satisfying answer be returned. All that can be said on the subject of the validity of Gurdjieff's teaching is that for *me* it has been the means of drawing together isolated parts of my experience – and I include ideas amongst these parts – so that they form a comprehensive whole. Thanks to the system my philosophy, religion and psychology are no longer, as they formerly were, disconnected scraps of knowledge, but integral parts of the general pattern of my thoughts. For me therefore the system is invaluable and bears the stamp of truth. Concerning its origin, very little can be stated, for Gurdjieff was deliberately vague whenever he was questioned on this subject. All that he would say was that he was not alone in his search for Ancient Knowledge, and that when he and his companions had found what they had been looking for, they fitted together their discoveries to form a self-consistent and coherent whole. This indicates that the system came from a number of different sources, and internal evidence strongly suggests that they were sources of a religious nature.

In his book, *Meetings with Remarkable Men*, Gurdjieff describes his journeys, his talks with dervishes and 'holy men', his visits to various monasteries and his admittance to certain ancient world brotherhoods. It was from these monasteries that he brought back his music and his sacred dances, and it is likely that they were the source of his knowledge as well. It is by symbols and rituals that truths of a religious nature are often expressed and many of the movements and dances he taught had a religious or philosophical significance. Some of the dances represented the movements of the planets round the sun, in accordance with the action of the two great cosmic laws, the law of three and the law of seven. Although Gurdjieff never actually stated that he had visited an Essene monastery, it is probable that he did so, for a French follower of his, who is also an authority on this subject, has discovered that there is a great similarity between the doctrines of this extremely ancient brotherhood and certain ideas of the system.

Gurdjieff's teaching has also affinities with Buddhism. Gurdjieff's pupils were required to turn the attention inwards and to watch the procession of thoughts, sensations and emotions which pass before them, forming a sequence of dissolving views in which one view fades into another, to be in turn replaced by yet another. If this experiment is carried out sincerely and without any preconceived ideas, no permanent and sovereign 'I' can be discovered, but only a sequence of fleeting 'I's, newly arising and as quickly disappearing. This conception of man, that he is not one but many, is the Buddhist conception of him. It is useless, says the Buddhist, for a man to search for anything in himself that exists by itself, that is 'independent and self-produced, unconnected with anything else'. It is useless for him to look for a veritable and permanent 'I' for no such 'I' exists. There is a Tibetan parable, quoted by Madame David-Neel, which illustrates the Buddhist view of man admirably. In it a 'person' is likened to a room in which a number of different people are meeting together to discuss how a certain problem shall be dealt with. One member of the meeting makes one proposal, another member suggests something else, a third something entirely different, and often two of them are on their feet and talking at the same time. At moments the discussion becomes so heated that there is a general disturbance and the meeting often ends in the interchange of blows.

The members of this assembly [writes Madame David-Neel] are the physical and mental elements which constitute the 'person'; they are our instincts, our tendencies, our ideas, our beliefs, our desires, etc. Through the causes which engendered them, each of them is the descendant and heir of many lines of causes, of many series of phenomena, going far back into the past, and whose traces are lost in the shadowy depths of eternity. (*Buddhism* (London, The Bodley Head, 1939) p. 131)

What could be closer than this to the account of man's many 'I's given by Mr Ouspensky at that first meeting described in this book?

Buddhism is not the only religion with which the system has affinities. There is a close relationship between the law of three as formulated by the system and the idea of the three *gunas* to be found in the Sankhya philosophy. According to this Indian philosophy, *prakriti*, or the creative force of Nature, is made up of three *gunas*, or principles. So long as these three principles remain in a state of equilibrium, nothing will happen, but when their equilibrium is disturbed by *purusha*, or spirit, they begin to create the diverse phenomena of nature. These three principles, or *gunas*, are known as Rajas, Tamas and Sattva, Rajas being the active, restless principle, Tamas the inert and enveloping principle and Sattva the light and illuminating principle. The *gunas* run like three twisted cords through the whole of Nature, and the different qualities to be found in different phenomena are said to be determined by which *guna* is predominant in them. But as Ouspensky pointed out to us, there is a difference in the account of the law of three as given by the system and as given by the Sankhya philosophy. According to the system a force may alter its character in different triads, for example, the neutralizing force in one triad may become the active force in the succeeding triad, whereas in the Sankhya philosophy each *guna* retains its distinctive qualities in whatever triad it happens to act. Ouspensky was of the opinion that the law of three, as expounded by the system, represented the original exposition of the three *gunas* and that in later editions of the Sankhya philosophy the account of them was altered. Whether this was the case or not, the law of three and the idea of the three *gunas* were almost certainly derived from a single and more ancient source.

The system also has many close affinities with Christianity and in his book, *In Search of the Miraculous*, Ouspensky reports a conversation with Gurdjieff in which he refers to the system as 'Esoteric Christianity'. Frequent references are made in the Gospels to the idea of sleep and of man's need for watchfulness, or, as the Greek word may be equally well rendered, wakefulness. Christ also told Nicodemus that it was necessary for man to be born again into a higher state of being and that before this could happen much of the old in him would have to die. In other words, he must free himself from a thousand petty attachments and identifications which hold him where he is. These harmful identifications keep alive in a man many 'I's which stand in the way of his evolution. Gurdjieff describes three stages in the freeing of a man from the useless part of himself, his false personality. The first stage in this liberating process was when he saw himself as he actually was, and not as he had always imagined himself to be; the second began when he fully realized his helplessness and his nothingness; the third when he had the courage and willingness to 'die', in other words, to renounce for ever what kept him in a state of servitude. There is a close similarity between this process of gaining freedom from the tyranny of the personality and the Christian idea of the death of the old Adam and the birth of the new. But as enunciated by the system, it is only that part of the personality which is imaginary or which is hostile to his development that has to die. The rest may survive, but instead of being active, as it has hitherto been, it must be rendered passive so that what is born anew in him may take control. Previously he has been ruled by his likes and dislikes, by his many identifications, by his petty conceits about himself, by the necessity of proving himself to be right, by the need for his merits to be recognized and by his desire for respect and appreciation. Henceforth he must renounce all such claims and, by doing this, liberate himself from what has hitherto held him in bondage. Only then will it be possible for him to reach a higher level of being and gain more knowledge.

This idea that a man's *knowledge* depends on his *being* is a central idea in the system. It is entirely foreign to all Western thought, for in the West a man's knowledge is looked upon as being determined only by his industry and by the acuteness of his intellect. Formerly knowledge was defined in broader terms as 'apprehended truth' but a much narrower meaning has now been given to this word. The fashionable school of Logical Positivist philosophy has gone so far as to make the word knowledge synonymous with scientific knowledge. Russell sums up the attitude of Logical Positivism to knowledge as follows:

> It regards philosophy as essentially one with science, differing from the special sciences merely by the generality of its problems ... It conceives that all knowledge is scientific knowledge, to be ascertained and proved by the methods of science. It does not aim, as previous philosophy has usually done, at statements about the universe as a whole, nor at the construction of a comprehensive system. It believes, on the basis of its logic, that there is no reason to deny the apparent piece-meal and higgledy-piggledy nature of the world. It does not regard the world as 'organic', in the sense that from any part adequately understood, the whole could be inferred, as the skeleton of an extinct monster can be inferred from a single bone.

I have quoted from Russell at length not only because his account of Logical Positivism shows the narrowness of the present view of knowledge, but because Logical Positivism is opposed to everything in the system. Those who belong to this school hold all metaphysical and religious statements to be meaningless and regard moral judgments as merely grunts of personal approval or disapproval of various forms of behaviour. The aim of Logical Positivism – if such a narrow system of thought can be said to have an aim – would seem to be to destroy all traditional knowledge and to divest everything in the Universe of any meaning. There could be no more unfortunate teaching in this spiritually bankrupt age.

It is unlikely that we shall ever know where Gurdjieff obtained his system of knowledge. Interesting though it would be to discuss its source it is quite possible that little would be gained by it. Forty years have passed since the Seekers of the Truth made their journeys through Turkestan, Afghanistan, Baluchistan and Tibet, and in the meantime much has happened in those regions. Barbarism is on the march, and by now many of the great monasteries in which Gurdjieff and his companions once stayed may have been destroyed, or, if not destroyed, been converted into barracks for Soviet troops. The ancient world brotherhoods he talked about may by now have been scattered or forced to retreat in small bands into still more remote and inaccessible regions before the advancing tide of modern 'civilization'. In the end barbarism invariably overcomes culture, but we have this at least for which to be thankful, that those to whom we owe this knowledge made their journeys before it was too late.

But what does it matter whether we know or not the origin of Gurdjieff's system of knowledge? The system stands or falls in accordance with its own intrinsic merits. We do not inquire into the credentials of the inventors of the wheel before using one, but are satisfied with the fact that it works.

EPILOGUE

Paris
30 May 1950

WHEN one is in the midst of events it is easy to lose one's sense of proportion and to invest certain happenings with an importance which they do not actually possess. Now that everything is over I have come across to Paris in order to obtain a bird's eye view of the past. It is easier to see the shape of yesterday than the shape of today, and by revisiting Rue des Colonels-Renard, the Salle Pleyel and other old Parisian haunts, I shall be able to view the past in better perspective. And it is only too true that everything is over, however unwilling I may be to acknowledge that it is so. The fact must be recognized that although we have much valuable material for further study, we shall receive nothing more unless – no, that conditional clause is superfluous, for to suppose that a group which has stumbled across a rivulet of knowledge, followed it for a while and then lost it, should rediscover it again higher up in its course, is so unlikely that it need not be considered. With the death of Gurdjieff this venture of mine has to come to an end.

A. has arranged to meet me in this literary rendezvous of the Latin quarter, but as I was early for my appointment, I have ordered coffee at a table in the sun. It was to this café that Ouspensky came whenever he visited Paris, and at this very table Gurdjieff himself may have sat wearing his astrakhan cap and with his gold-mounted cane resting against this chair. It is fitting therefore that A. and I should have arranged to meet at this café, not only because of its links with our teachers, but on account of its name, 'Le Café des Deux Magots', the coffee-house of the two grotesques! What could be more appropriate? I have long accepted the fact that my professional colleagues would dub me an 'antic fellow' if they were to discover the nature of my psychological and philosophical researches during the last twenty years. In imagination I can hear them ask, 'On whose authority do you accept these wild statements that man is asleep and unable to "do"? What experimental evidence can you put forward in support of these ideas? And if to these questions I were to reply that both my authority and my evidence were strong enough to satisfy all scientific requirements, they would either smile or frown and then pass quickly to some other subject. Unconventionality in thought is as distressing as unconventionality in dress to the polite and well-regulated mind.

This pavement soliloquy of mine has been brought to an end by the arrival of A. He has been longer than I in Paris and in closer touch with Gurdjieff's followers, but I will give him time to order his drink before I put to him any question.

'Have you any news?' I ask of him as soon as his Dubonnet has arrived.

'About what?'

'About the papers Gurdjieff left behind. Did they contain any hint as to the source of his knowledge?'

'Nothing at all.'

'Then we can assume,' I continued, 'that the system was derived from many sources, and particularly from that monastery he describes in the mountainous regions of Turkestan. You remember that Gurdjieff once told Ouspensky that schools were divided up into philosophical, theoretical and practical schools, and that practical schools were to be found only in Persia, Mesopotamia and Turkestan. Well, the system is obviously practical, and that is why I have always been particularly interested in that journey of Gurdjieff's to a remote monastery in Turkestan.'

A. was a long time in answering me. 'It's only a guess,' he said, 'and we can't even be sure that the world brotherhood he writes about actually exists. Some of the journeys he describes and the people he meets were probably only literary devices by means of which certain ideas could be given. He seems to suggest that he is going to use them for that purpose in the introduction to his second series of books. Besides, there is other evidence in support of this. You remember Prince Lubovedsky – whom he met at various times, and once at that very monastery you've just been talking about – well, R. tells me that the name Lubovedsky is made up of two Russian words meaning "love of knowledge".

The Prince is therefore either a purely fictitious character, or else a composite figure, representative of several people, including possibly Gurdjieff himself.'

'That description of the River Amu-Darya is so convincing and he gives so many details that are not really required by the story that I find it quite impossible to believe that Gurdjieff never actually saw it.'

'I agree,' answered A. quietly, 'and I did not for a moment suggest that *Meetings with Remarkable Men* was a work of fiction. I only said that, like all other writers, Gurdjieff creates the situations he needs for the best presentation of his ideas. I am sure at any rate of one thing. If Gurdjieff had meant us to try to get into touch after his death with those from whom he obtained his knowledge, he would have left us more explicit instructions than are to be found in his book. As he has given us nothing on which we can act, we must conclude that he did not intend this.'

'Then you feel as I do,' I said, 'that the whole thing is finished.'

A. nodded his head, hesitated, and then added, but in so low a voice that I had difficulty in hearing him, 'Unless, of course, some move is made by *them*.'

Here was something I never even considered and yet what A. had said was not unreasonable. We knew that somewhere there existed people with knowledge that does not find its way into books, and it was probable that it was still being handed down to those who were ready to receive it. 'You haven't given up all hope of finding more?' I said.

'I haven't,' A. answered. 'It's true that we've been given no clue and no longer have a teacher, but our situation is much better than it was before.'

'You mean that we have a touchstone by means of which to separate the true from the false?'

'We have even more than that. We may again be seekers, but we are seekers who have found much of which we have not yet made full use. We have lost our teacher, but, as Gurdjieff once told Ouspensky, in such circumstances the most experienced of the pupils becomes the teacher. It is not as though we had been deprived of all help. You know what I mean.'

I nodded.

'Let's have a final drink,' said A. breaking the long silence which ensued. 'What's yours?'

'A small glass of red vodka, if they've got it,' I answered.

A. looked surprised and then said, 'You've acquired a taste for it, I see.'

'No, I still dislike it but – well, vodka is linked up in my mind with certain memories and this happens to be a moment in which I wish to drink it.'

And when we had had and paid for our drinks, we made our way together along the Boulevard St Germain in the direction of our hotel.

PARIS

The Arc de Triomphe

PARIS

The Arc de Triomphe

INCREDI
BUILDS

IncrediBuilds, A Division of Insight Editions, LP

INTRODUCTION

Intended to surpass the impressive triumphal arches of ancient Rome, the Arc de Triomphe originated as a part of Napoleon's grandiose plan for Paris. Today it stands as one of the world's largest and best-known monuments.

The Arc de Triomphe first honored the victory of Napoleon's Grande Armée over Russian and Austrian armies in the Battle of Austerlitz, but Napoleon never saw the Arc completed. King Louis-Philippe of France finished construction thirty years after work began, after Napoleon's death. The majestic arch maintains its status as a symbol of France today, standing at the end of the Champs Élysées, one of the world's most famous and beautiful streets.

FACTS & FIGURES

- *Construction started:* 1806
- *Completed:* 1836
- *Architects:* Jean François Thérèse Chalgrin and Guillaume Abel Blouet
- *Height:* 162 feet (49.5 meters)
- *Width:* 148 feet (45 meters)

- *Location:* Center of Place Charles de Gaulle/Place de l'Étoile, at the end of the Champs-Élysées
- *Inspiration:* 1st century Roman Arch of Titus
- *Original purpose:* To honor the triumph of Napoleon's Grande Armée at Austerlitz in 1805

- *Current purpose:* Honoring France and the sacrifices of French soldiers throughout history
- *Cost to build:* 9.3 million French francs in 1836, or approximately 90 million euros today

Paris, 1806

After the chaos of the ten-year French Revolution, France looked to ancient Rome for inspiration to build a new city and society. Almost two thousand years after Caesar became Emperor of Rome, Napoleon became Emperor of France. In art, culture, fashion, and government, Napoleon led a neoclassical revolution. Some of the beauty and grace of today's classic Parisian boulevards came from the inspiration the Napoleonic era took from the Rome of the Caesars.

The French Revolution had devastated France's aristocracy and disrupted Paris's population and lifestyle. As emperor, Napoleon began building projects to bring the city under a new order. The Louvre became a museum instead of a palace. Many of Paris's boulevards were widened or beautified, and bridges were built to connect the city, including the first iron bridge over the Seine.

GETTING AROUND

In 1806, there were no cars or trains. Parisians promenaded on foot in the public and private gardens of the Palais-Royal, the early 19th century version of the collection of shops and restaurants found along today's Champs-Élysées. The Palais-Royal was the center of fashion, entertainment, food, and culture during Napoleon's time as emperor.

CULTURAL SCENE

"Everything in Paris is about fashion and fantasy," wrote a German visitor in 1807. Fashionable Parisians could show their style and grace while shopping for any type of luxury item they desired, especially on the Boulevard des Italiens and Boulevard du Temple. They could also promenade and enjoy the scenery in the Gardens of Tivoli, named for the famous gardens in Rome. Located in the modern-day neighborhood of Saint-Lazare, the Gardens featured amusements, parks of various styles, theaters, and street entertainers.

EMPIRE DRESSES
Today's Empire waist dresses are inspired by fashions of the Napoleonic Empire. The high waist, flowing fabric, and ultra-feminine look were modeled on ancient Roman and Greek clothing, a taste adopted by Napoleon's first empress, Josephine de Beauharnais, and her daughter from her first marriage, Hortense, as well as other fashionable French women.

A SAFER, HEALTHIER PARIS

After Napoleon crowned himself emperor, he told his Minister of the Interior, scientist Jean-Antoine Chaptal, "I want to do something great and useful for Paris." Chaptal said, "If so, give it water." Diseases wracked the city throughout the French Revolution, but by 1806, Parisian families were healthier because of the new sewers and better water supply built by Napoleon.

Napoleon Bonaparte:

FROM CORSICA TO AUSTERLITZ

Napoleon Bonaparte gave his name to an Empire, military theories, history, and even a dessert.

Born in 1769 on the Mediterranean island of Corsica to parents of noble, but not wealthy, Tuscan ancestry, Napoleon attended school in France and joined the French military shortly after his graduation in 1785. Only four years later, in 1789, the French Revolution began.

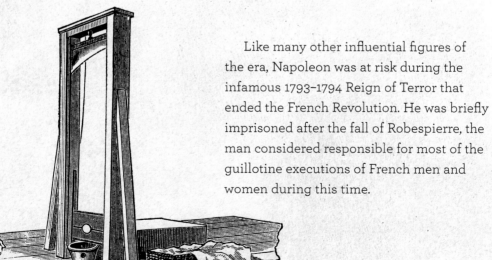

Like many other influential figures of the era, Napoleon was at risk during the infamous 1793–1794 Reign of Terror that ended the French Revolution. He was briefly imprisoned after the fall of Robespierre, the man considered responsible for most of the guillotine executions of French men and women during this time.

NAPOLEON'S FIRST ARMY

By the end of the French Revolution, Napoleon was released from prison and was made a brigadier general. One of his first actions was to save the new French Republican government by firing cannons at a Royalist mob at the Siege of Toulon. He was only twenty-six years old when the grateful government gave him command of the Army of Italy. He began a series of

campaigns that, within five years, resulted in victories over Egypt, Austria, Italy, and many other European forces. In 1804, after Napoleon had spent four years as a Consul of the Republic, Pope Pius VII crowned Napoleon the Emperor of France in a grand ceremony in the great Notre Dame Cathedral in Paris. Napoleon then crowned his beloved wife, Josephine, as empress.

Soon, the Napoleonic Wars began, during which Napoleon sought to control all of Europe. Napoleon's greatest victory came in December 1805 at Austerlitz. In the Battle of Austerlitz, also called "The Battle of the Three Emperors," the French defeated larger Austrian and Russian forces. This is considered one of the greatest tactical military victories of all time.

WHAT DID HE REALLY SAY?

Many things Napoleon never said became linked to him. Still, he had many interesting *real* quotes. Here are some of his most famous:
- "The best way to keep one's word is not to give it."
- "A leader is a dealer in hope."
- "He who fears being conquered is sure of defeat."

Victory Construction Projects

Although he never saw it completed, the Arc de Triomphe represents Napoleon Bonaparte's ambition to make Paris a greater world capital than Caesar's Rome. The Arc de Triomphe was first designed to celebrate Napoleon's greatest military triumph, the Battle of Austerlitz. It was just one of many Napoleonic-era projects celebrating military victories. It was one of the grandest, however, intended to be more than twice the height of its inspiration, the Arch of Titus in Rome. Napoleon decreed that the Arc would act as a triumphal entry to the heart of Paris.

In March 1806, Napoleon gave neoclassical architect Jean-François-Thérèse Chalgrin the task of designing the new triumphal arch and finding the best location. Two months later, the Place de l'Étoile was chosen. However, after two years, only the foundations had been completed. Four years later, a version of the Arc de Triomphe—made of painted canvas and wood—was raised to celebrate Napoleon's marriage to his second wife, Empress Maria Louise of Austria.

THE VENDOME COLUMN

Ancient Egypt's obelisks provided another inspiration for Napoleonic-era architects and artists. Like the Arc de Triomphe, the Egyptian-inspired Vendôme Column was designed to honor Napoleon's victory at the Battle of Austerlitz. Completed in 1805 and made from over 1,800 melted artillery pieces captured from Russian and Austrian forces, the column has been vandalized and rebuilt more than once due to political changes. Famous French author Honoré de Balzac wrote that Paris had a "great mast, made entirely of bronze," while equally famous author Victor Hugo wrote a poem about King Louis XVIII's vandalism of the column's crowning statue of Napoleon, which was eventually restored in 1871.

LOUISIANA PURCHASE
In 1803, Napoleon sold the Louisiana territory (828,000 square miles) to the United States for $15 million to raise funds for wars and construction projects, including the Arc de Triomphe.

THE ELEPHANT OF THE BASTILLE

One of the most famous and whimsical Napoleonic-era monuments is the Elephant of the Bastille. Napoleon began building a giant elephant statue to commemorate the famous Storming of the Bastille, the event that began the French Revolution. A 78-foot-tall (24-meter) hollow plaster model of the elephant was completed in 1814, but plans for the final bronze structure stopped after Napoleon's defeat at the Battle of Waterloo. The model stood, decaying, near the Bastille's former location for another thirty years, and was featured as a shelter for street children in Victor Hugo's famous novel, *Les Misérables*.

Military Action

Throughout his reign, Napoleon experienced both great victories like Austerlitz, and great defeats like the 1805 Battle of Trafalgar that wiped out the French Navy.

The longer he remained emperor, the more countries Napoleon invaded, until in 1812, he chose to invade Russia with 600,000 troops. The invasion resulted in a catastrophic defeat, and only 100,000 French troops returned home. Napoleon also lost to Spanish, Portuguese, and British troops, and eventually, France was invaded by a coalition of Russian, Austrian, Prussian (German), and Swedish troops. In May 1814, Paris fell to this coalition and Napoleon was forced to abdicate his throne and was sent into exile on the island of Elba near the Italian coast. The French monarchy was then restored under Louis XVIII, the grandson of Louis XV.

NAPOLEON'S RETURN

Napoleon lived in exile on Elba for less than a year, plotting his escape and return to France. In February 1815, Napoleon escaped and returned to France with one thousand supporters. He was greeted by cheering crowds in Paris. Louis XVIII fled; Napoleon then began his second reign as Emperor of France, called the Hundred Days.

THE HUNDRED DAYS

Napoleon's army won a battle against Prussian forces on June 16, 1815. Two days later, near the village of Waterloo, 72,000 French troops marched against 68,000 British, German, and Belgian troops commanded by the Duke of Wellington. Reported to be exhausted and in poor health, Napoleon made military errors as he never had before. More than 33,000 out of the original 72,000 French troops died, were wounded, or were taken prisoner at Waterloo. Four days later, Napoleon abdicated the throne again and was exiled to an island so remote he would have no chance of escaping this time: Saint Helena, 2,500 miles east of Brazil and 1,200 miles west of Africa, in the middle of the south Atlantic. There, Napoleon died in 1821 at age fifty-one, a lonely and broken man.

SURPRISING FACTS ABOUT THE BATTLE OF WATERLOO

1. Napoleon never set foot in Waterloo, according to Belgian historian Bernard Coppens. The battle was fought about three miles south of the town, near Mont Saint-Jean.

2. Despite being led by the British Duke of Wellington, very few British troops fought in the battle. The forces were primarily German, Dutch, and Belgian. A separate Prussian army also fought.

3. The first place Napoleon considered for his escape after defeat was the United States. A British blockade of the French coast prevented this, and he was eventually captured and sent to the island of St. Helena, one of the most remote locations in the world.

The Last French King Completes the Arc

The Arc de Triomphe was only partially finished at the time Napoleon was forced to abdicate his throne in 1814 .

It remained unfinished until the reign of Louis-Philippe I (1830–1848). The last French monarch of the House of Orléans, Louis-Philippe, was initially popular with the French people, and was called the "bourgeois king." His father, Philippe Égalité ("equality"), styled himself as a man of the people during the French Revolution, but still lost his life to the guillotine. Louis-Philippe became increasingly criticized during his reign; he was even portrayed as an uncaring figure in the French media.

After three years as king, Louis-Philippe restarted construction on the Arc de Triomphe. This time, he dedicated the monument not just to Napoleon's victory at Austerlitz, but to the French armed forces throughout history. Architect Guillaume Blouet completed the work, which was engraved with the names of 660 people, including 558 French generals of the First Empire. Visitors will notice that some of the generals' names are underlined, which means that they died in battle. Large sculptural reliefs by famous French sculptors adorn each of the massive columns. Together, the sculptures, their style, and the Arc itself represent the style of romantic neoclassicism, echoing the spirit of Greece and Rome, but also of 19th- century France.

In another gesture of generosity, Louis-Philippe brought Napoleon's remains back to Paris from the island of St. Helena, where they were buried with many of France's other great military leaders at the military hospital of Les Invalides in 1840.

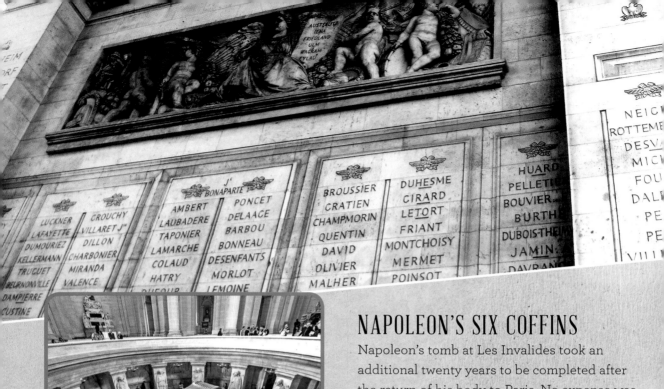

NAPOLEON'S SIX COFFINS

Napoleon's tomb at Les Invalides took an additional twenty years to be completed after the return of his body to Paris. No expense was spared: his body is contained within six layered coffins made of iron, mahogany, two of lead, ebony, with the final exterior coffin made of red porphyry. These are displayed on a granite pedestal surrounded by twelve victory pillars.

LES INVALIDES

Les Invalides is a large group of buildings, courtyards, and gardens in Central Paris that includes the original Hôpital des Invalides built by King Louis XIV in 1670. Begun as a hospital for soldiers and a home for retired veterans, Les Invalides is not only the site of Napoleon's tomb, but also includes the tombs of several of his family members and of other French military heroes. A dramatic statue of Napoleon overlooks the cour d'honneur, the largest of fifteen courts that once hosted military parades.

Art & Cultural Influences

T he Arc de Triomphe is modeled after Rome's Arch of Titus. Located near the Roman Forum, the Arch of Titus still stands today, with its sculptured reliefs depicting triumphs like the Emperor Titus' defeat of Jerusalem, including captured Jewish temple art such as the seven-branched menorah.

The Arch of Titus has two massive columns featuring deep relief sculptures on either side of a high arched passage. In Rome, victory parades were called "triumphs." Captured enemy soldiers, spoils of war such as gold and silver, and even unusual animals like giraffes or lions were paraded through arches.

ROMANTIC NEOCLASSICISM

Not just Napoleon, but all of Europe and America were interested in the art, government, philosophy, and learning of ancient Greece and Rome.

Before the neoclassical period, art and architecture had been very elaborate, featuring the Baroque and Rococo styles. The enormous palace of Versailles is an example of Baroque French architecture. Times changed and tastes grew simpler, and classical buildings excavated in Pompeii and Athens gave Europeans a better idea of Roman and Greek architecture.

The simplicity of Roman columns and domes, and the elegant, flowing gowns worn by the women depicted in Greek statues inspired the aesthetic of the period. Romantic elements were introduced to the style by Eugène Delacroix, who painted *Liberty Leading the People*. While the Arc de Triomphe itself is neoclassical, the relief sculptures on each side of the base are much more similar to the romantic images painted by Delacroix. Still, France was always the center of neoclassical painting. Its most famous painter of the movement was Jacques-Louis David, who became Napoleon's official painter.

Another of France's greatest painters was Jean Auguste Dominique Ingres, who incorporated elements of different artistic styles of the past into his work. His neoclassical portrait of Napoleon as an emperor in his coronation robes was painted in 1806, at the same time as the Arc de Triomphe was originally being planned.

ARCHITECTURE

GOTHIC

FRENCH BAROQUE

NEOCLASSICAL

Art of the Arc de Triomphe

By 1823, when Louis-Philippe restarted the construction of the Arc de Triomphe, romanticism had become popular in Europe.

Romanticism is a movement of art, writing, music, culture, and fashion that began at the end of the 18th century and continued for another fifty years. Hallmarks of romanticism include imagination and emotion in painting, sculpture, and music. Scenes of man's struggle against nature and extreme emotion are common, as well as an interest in individual appearance, nature, and emotional states.

THE DEPARTURE OF THE VOLUNTEERS OF 1792

La Marseillaise, or *The Departure of the Volunteers of 1792*, by François Rude is the most famous sculpture on the Arc de Triomphe, and it has a place of honor on one of the front columns looking to the Champs-Élysées. The sculpture commemorates the Battle of Valmy, during which French volunteers defended the Republic against an attack by Austrian and Prussian forces. The central figure is the bold military figure of the "Genius of Liberty," represented as a winged, sword-bearing woman. Yet the sculpture is not completely romantic in style. Rude included the neoclassical trait of balanced figures and symbols on both sides to create symmetry in the composition. He based Liberty's wings on the classic Greek statue of Nike of Samothrace called *Winged Victory*, today found in the Louvre. The French soldiers in *La Marseillaise* are nude, similar to classical Greek and Roman sculptures, while the opposing Germans are bearded and wearing armor.

THE TRIUMPH OF 1810

The sculpture on the other column, facing the Champs-Élysées, is a more classically-styled depiction of Napoleon. As Rude did in *La Marseillaise*, sculptor Jean-Pierre Cortot used symmetry to balance the figures on each side of Napoleon, who wears classical Greek robes. The sculpture shows Napoleon being crowned by the goddess of Victory, surrounded by other figures that represent Liberty, Faith, and Learning. The figures celebrate the Treaty of Vienna, which imposed harsh peace terms on Austria. Austria ceded territory to Bavaria, the Russian Empire, and France. The different territories are represented symbolically through the clothing of the different female figures surrounding Napoleon.

Art of the Arc de Triomphe Continued

THE RESISTANCE OF 1814

On the western facade of the Arc are two sculptures by Antoine Étex. The first is called *The Resistance of 1814*, or *War*, and is a symbolic representation of the attack of allied British, Prussian, and Russian forces on France in 1814. Female and male figures representing vulnerable French people beg for help and cling to the legs of a heroic soldier who stands in the center of the sculpture. The battles are represented by a horse and its rider, who leans back in action as if he has been struck by a blow. A winged female representing Victory leans over the group, watching for signs of victory or defeat.

THE PEACE OF 1815

The Peace of 1815, or *Paix*, is the second sculpture completed by Étex for the Arc. This sculpture depicts Justice overlooking the French people, who are shown sowing wheat, caring for a child, and upholding the torch of Liberty. The sculpture depicts the aftermath of the Treaty of Paris, signed by the French government after Napoleon's defeat at the Battle of Waterloo. The figures representing French men and women are shown with expressions of exhaustion and defeat, while the central French soldier has his head bowed. He does not look defeated, but he no longer looks ready to fight.

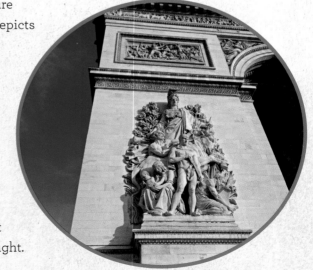

RELIEF FAÇADES

Six rectangular friezes sculpted in high relief adorn the Arc above the large sculptures on the pillars and on each side façade. These sculptures are complex, depicting five French battle victories and the burial of General Marceau, the most famous general during the French Revolutionary Wars.

Of the depicted battles, the Battle of Aboukir and Fall of Alexandria (Egypt), the Battle of Arcole (Italy), and the Battle of Austerlitz were fought by Napoleon, while the Battle of Jemappes (Belgium) was fought during the French Revolutionary War.

In addition to the large friezes on each side of the Arc, there are dozens of smaller reliefs and friezes, each depicting a different aspect of French military history or culture. Beneath the arch are not only the names of the Napoleonic-era generals and others who sacrificed their lives, but many other beautiful sculptures and reliefs in neoclassical and romantic styles as well.

INTERIOR PILLARS AND CEILING

The interior of the Arc includes the names of the greatest battles of the French Revolution and the Napoleonic Wars. Victories are also engraved, as are lists of Revolutionary and Napoleonic generals. The ceiling is decorated with twenty-one sculpted roses inlaid in a geometric design. Inside, the Arc also includes a monument to French soldiers of the First World War, and an exhibition about its design and construction.

Tomb of the Unknown Soldier

After the First World War, the Tomb of the Unknown Soldier and the Eternal Flame were added.

The Tomb of the Unknown Soldier represents a newer era of conflict and victory for France than the time of Napoleon or Louis-Philippe. It is one of three memorials built by the Allies after World War I, which was fought between 1914 and 1918—a hundred years after the Battle of Waterloo.

FORMER ENEMIES, NOW ALLIES

Britain had been France's bitter enemy during the Napoleonic Wars, in which the British Duke of Wellington defeated Napoleon at Waterloo. However, by World War I, France, Britain, and the United States were allies in the conflict against Germany and Austria-Hungary. Following the end of the First World War, the idea emerged in all three Allied countries to honor those who had died in the war by burying an unknown soldier discovered on the battlefield.

Two unknown soldiers were interred simultaneously in Paris and London on November 11, 1920, called Armistice Day. The date marks the anniversary of the end of World War I in 1918.

In London, the soldier was buried in the Tomb of the Unknown Warrior in Westminster Abbey.

In Paris, the soldier was buried at the Arc de Triomphe in the Tomb of the Unknown Soldier.

One year later, an American soldier was buried in the Tomb of the Unknown Soldier overlooking Arlington National Cemetery near Washington, D.C., also on Armistice Day (today celebrated in the United States as Veterans Day).

Later, the Eternal Flame honoring those who died in World War I and World War II was lit at the Arc de Triomphe. It has burned everyday since November 11, 1923. Eternal flames have been used throughout history to commemorate important events or to honor soldiers or leaders.

The Eternal Flame at the Tomb of the Unknown Soldier at the Arc de Triomphe is thought to be the oldest, longest-burning eternal flame in Europe. It is maintained by the Committee of the Flame, which coordinates more than eighty volunteer organizations. Volunteer groups make sure the flame is lit and conduct the ceremonies in memory of the soldiers who died. Every evening at 6:30 p.m., volunteers rekindle the Eternal Flame and lay red, white, and blue wreaths of the French tricolor flag in memory of the French people who have perished in war.

France Today

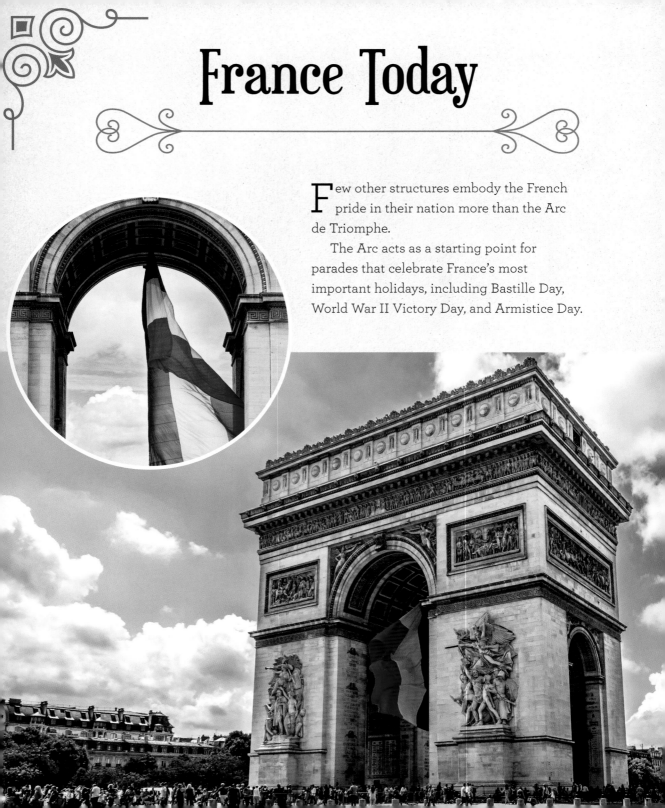

Few other structures embody the French pride in their nation more than the Arc de Triomphe.

The Arc acts as a starting point for parades that celebrate France's most important holidays, including Bastille Day, World War II Victory Day, and Armistice Day.

CHAMPS ÉLYSÉES AND PLACE DE GAULLE

Originating in the late 16th century as a promenade and park-like extension of the gardens of the Tuileries Palace, today's Champs-Élysées is only 1.2 miles (1.9 kilometers)

long. It is one of the world's most famous streets, running between the Place de la Concorde and the Place Charles de Gaulle, which surrounds the Arc de Triomphe. Its name echoes Ancient Greece's mythological paradise, the Elysian Fields. By the mid-19th century, the Champs-Élysées was already lined with dozens of fashionable stores, and today is the location of some of the world's most upscale shopping. It hosts the flagship stores of luxury brands including Louis Vuitton, Lacoste, Hugo Boss, and Cartier. The Élysée Palace, home of France's president, is located just off the Champs-Élysées.

The Arc de Triomphe is located in the center of the Place de L'Étoile, or Square of the Star, which is the circular junction of twelve of Paris's greatest avenues, including the Champs-Élysées. The Place de L'Étoile, also called Place Charles de Gaulle, can be found in guides and maps, and the names are used interchangeably. Place Charles de Gaulle honors France's great World War II general and president. The junction is also the center of Paris's ten-kilometer *Axe historique*, or historical axis, which

begins at the Louvre and terminates in Paris's high rise district La Défense. A modern triumphal arch commemorating humanity and peace, the Grande Arche de La Défense, is the western end of the *Axe historique*.

FAMOUS FLIGHT

In 1919, French World War I pilot Charles Godefroy became famous for flying his biplane through the Arc de Triomphe after France's Victory Parade celebrating the end of the First World War. Godefroy performed his famous flight after being grounded for the victory parade—he and fellow WWI aces were told they had to march on foot alongside the other soldiers.

Arc de Triomphe Today

Many people believe that the best view of Paris is from the top of the Eiffel Tower, but the Arc de Triomphe offers unparalleled views from its top, each direction offering a different view along the twelve avenues that comprise the "star" in the heart of the Place de l'Étoile.

Some visitors may want to take an elevator to the top, but the Arc de Triomphe also has an amazing 284-step spiral staircase that leads to a small museum about the monument's construction before ending at the top gallery.

VISITOR INFORMATION

Admirers can view the Arc de Triomphe from ground level on foot or by car or bus. Admission is free for visitors under age seventeen. Visitors are advised to enter the Arc itself by the underground tunnel on the Avenue de la Grande Armée side of the circle. The eternal flame at the Tomb of the Unknown Soldier is rekindled every evening at 6:30 p.m.

Closed only on major French Holidays (Christmas, New Year, May 1, May 8, July 14, and November 11), the Arc is open until 11:00 p.m. during the summer months and 10:30 p.m. the rest of the year.

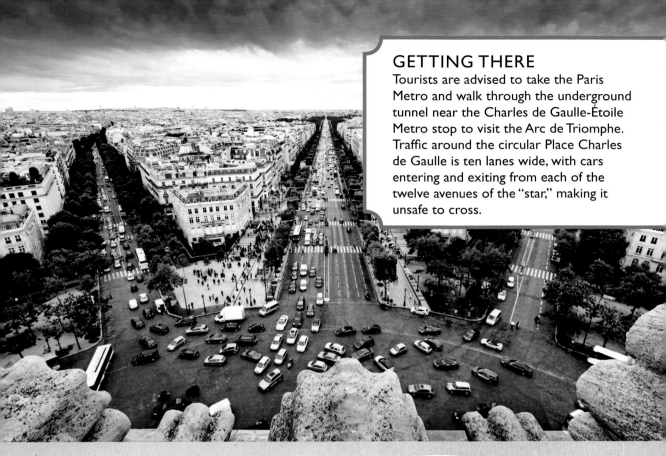

GETTING THERE

Tourists are advised to take the Paris Metro and walk through the underground tunnel near the Charles de Gaulle-Étoile Metro stop to visit the Arc de Triomphe. Traffic around the circular Place Charles de Gaulle is ten lanes wide, with cars entering and exiting from each of the twelve avenues of the "star," making it unsafe to cross.

TOUR DE FRANCE

The most famous bicycle race in the world, the Tour de France, is a 2,200-mile-long (3,500-kilometer) race throughout France that includes twenty-one stages, ending with the final sprint down the Champs-Élysées to the Arc de Triomphe. Often called "the world's largest sporting event," the Tour takes twenty-three days to complete. Some stages of the race may take place outside of France, and in the past have been held in England, Belgium, and Switzerland—but the race always ends at the Arc de Triomphe.

Make It Your Own

One of the great things about IncrediBuilds™ models is that each one is completely customizable. The untreated, natural wood can be decorated with paints, pencils, pens, beads, sequins—the list goes on and on!

Before you start building and decorating your model, read through the included instruction sheet so you understand how all the pieces come together. Then, choose a theme and make a plan. Do you want to make an exact replica of the Arc de Triomphe, or something different? The choice is yours! Here are some sample projects to get those creative juices flowing.

IN THE DAYTIME

The Arc de Triomphe stands brightly as a brilliant neoclassical marvel. Try your hand at using various shades of gray to add some depth to your model.

WHAT YOU NEED:
- Paintbrush
- Four different shades of gray paint—from very light to dark

WHAT YOU MIGHT WANT:
- Water-based gouache paint

GOAUCHE PAINT is a type of opaque watercolor. It blends nicely and coats the wood well. If you don't have gouache, acrylic paint will work too.

1. After assembling the model, paint the entire model the lightest shade of gray you have.

2. Next, use a slightly darker shade of gray to outline the sculptural artwork on all sides of the model and above the arch. This doesn't need to be precise—just start blocking the art. You can also add some paint to the edges of the bricks at random intervals.

3. Next, using that same shade of gray, paint the following:
   - The base of each pillar
   - The sides of the archways
   - The outer portion of the circles at the top
   - The long bricks under the circles
   - The upper eave
   - The stripe above the circle

4. Go back and paint the edges of the artwork with an even darker gray to add shadows.

5. You'll also want to add shadows in these spots. (See letters on model to the left.)
   a. Shadows in the circles
   b. Shadows in the stones on the arch ways
   c. Shadows in the upper left of the little squares at the top

6. Finally, go back and add the darkest shadows you want on all of the art.

7. Add the darkest paint to these spots too. (See letters on model to the left.)
   d. The inner frames
   e. Edges of tiered horizontal stripes
   f. Lower right of the small squares on top

Play around as you create the shadows. Make things darker or lighter depending on your preference.

AFTER DARK

They don't call it the City of Light for nothing! After dark, the Arc de Triomphe lights up and stands as a beacon on the end of the Champs-Élysées.

WHAT YOU NEED:
- Paintbrush
- Yellow and orange paint
- Red-brown, yellow, orange-yellow, and orange colored pencils

TIP:
Color all of the pieces *before* you build the model.

PIECES 29-32

The light on the Arc de Triomphe typically shines from the ground up, casting shadows as you near the top. The square top section is indented on the real Arc de Triomphe and receives the most shadows at night. Color this section red-brown to illustrate those shadows. You may even want to add another layer of regular brown on top to blend. Keep the edges yellow and orange, or a blend of the two.

THE MAIN ARCHWAY PANELS
(PIECES 1, 2, 4, 5)

1. Color these pieces yellow to start.

2. Blend some orange-yellow into the bricks and around the artwork.

3. Outline the artwork in red-brown and shade some shadows around the top of each.

4. Use orange to outline the arch and artwork frames.

5. Use the red-brown to color in more shadows. A light shading on the edges of the panels will help to add depth.

BLENDING
Use colored pencils to blend by carefully laying colors on top of each other, much the same way as you would with paint.

TO FINISH

Make sure the rest of the pieces are colored in how you like then assemble the model. Paint the wooden edges of the model a blend of yellow and orange. You can paint the interior and the base of each pillar another color if you would like. A dark blue was used here to represent night.

THE FRENCH FLAG

Often, the French flag hangs in the center of the Arc de Triomphe, so why not try your hand at recreating the flag with your model?

WHAT YOU NEED:
- Paint brush
- Red, white, and blue acrylic paint
- Painter's tape

1. Start by dividing the model into thirds.

2. Use the painter's tape to outline the middle section. Paint the middle section white and let dry.

3. Carefully peel off the tape.

4. Next, cover the white section with tape so there are clean lines on either side.

5. Paint the left side blue.

6. Paint the right side red. Let dry.

7. Carefully peel off the tape.

8. If there are any mistakes from the tape, just touch them up with a small brush.

A SKETCH

Try this project that takes the simple art of a quick sketch and makes it 3D.

WHAT YOU NEED:
- Paintbrush
- White or cream-colored paint
- Fine-tipped black marker

1. Paint the entire model white. Let dry.

2. Take the black marker and slowly sketch in the details using the engravings as a guide. Take your time. Don't worry if it's messy—this is a rough sketch.

If you would like your model to appear more like a charcoal sketch, drag a wet paintbrush through the marker lines to the paint to add more smudge marks.

IncrediBuilds™
A Division of Insight Editions, LP
San Rafael, CA 94912
www.incredibuilds.com
www.insighteditions.com

f Find us on Facebook: www.facebook.com/
    InsightEditions
🐦 Follow us on Twitter: @insighteditions

Published in 2017 by Insight Editions, LP, San Rafael,
California. All rights reserved. No part of this book may be
reproduced in any form without written permission from
the publisher.

Copyright © 2017 by Insight Editions, LP

Library of Congress Cataloging-in-Publication Data
available.

ISBN 978-1-68298-072-9

Publisher: Raoul Goff
Art Director: Chrissy Kwasnik
Designer: Brie Brewer and Leah Bloise
Executive Editor: Vanessa Lopez
Project Editor: Rebekah Piatte
Managing Editor: Alan Kaplan
Production Editor: Lauren LePera
Editorial Assistant: Erum Khan
Production Coordinator: Sam Taylor
Model Designer: Zihang Wu, TeamGreen

Manufactured in China

10 9 8 7 6 5 4 3 2 1

ROOTS of PEACE 🌐 REPLANTED PAPER

Insight Editions, in association with Roots of Peace, will
plant two trees for each tree used in the manufacturing of
this book. Roots of Peace is an internationally renowned
humanitarian organization dedicated to eradicating land
mines worldwide and converting war-torn lands into
productive farms and wildlife habitats. Roots of Peace
will plant two million fruit and nut trees in Afghanistan
and provide farmers there with the skills and support
necessary for sustainable land use.